To my §[...]
enjoy the read !

Dick / Dunderson

5 - 18 - 12

RICHARD L. GUNDERSON, CFA

A FEW GOOD EGGS IN ONE BASKET

The Power of a Concentrated
Portfolio of Common Stocks

iUniverse, Inc.
Bloomington

A Few Good Eggs in One Basket
The Power of a Concentrated Portfolio of Common Stocks

The information, ideas, and suggestions in this book are not intended to render professional advice. Before following any suggestions contained in this book, you should consult your personal accountant or other financial advisor. Neither the author nor the publisher shall be liable or responsible for any loss or damage allegedly arising as a consequence of your use or application of any information or suggestions in this book.

iUniverse books may be ordered through booksellers or by contacting:

iUniverse
1663 Liberty Drive
Bloomington, IN 47403
www.iuniverse.com
1-800-Authors (1-800-288-4677)

Because of the dynamic nature of the Internet, any Web addresses or links contained in this book may have changed since publication and may no longer be valid. The views expressed in this work are solely those of the author and do not necessarily reflect the views of the publisher, and the publisher hereby disclaims any responsibility for them.

Any people depicted in stock imagery provided by Thinkstock are models, and such images are being used for illustrative purposes only.

Certain stock imagery © Thinkstock.

ISBN: 978-1-4697-7171-7 (sc)
ISBN: 978-1-4697-7173-1 (hc)
ISBN: 978-1-4697-7172-4 (e)

Printed in the United States of America

iUniverse rev. date: 4/17/2012

Acknowledgments

This book has been too long in the making. The outline for *A Few Eggs in One Basket* began to take shape over a decade ago, but even before then, the desire to write a book about investing had emerged and persisted. However, for a variety of reasons, including procrastination and doubts about what to say and how to say it, weeks turned into months, and months into years.

The main regret I have is not finishing the book a few years ago. In hindsight, I can see that a finished book may have resulted in my avoiding a few major mistakes. Warren Buffett has stated repeatedly that a basic tenet of successful investing is avoiding the big loss. I erred in not recognizing that when a corporation makes a large acquisition for cash that results in a highly leveraged balance sheet, the risk profile changes significantly, and the attribute of financial vitality is violated. But for a big loss or two, I'm confident the investment return of my portfolio would have exceeded the average annual return of an index fund over a period of twenty years.

I want to thank all of the people who have encouraged me to write (and complete) this book. Some of them have said they want their own copies to read and keep in their personal libraries—but we'll see how they react once they get a glimpse of what I've been up to for all these years. But at the very least, friends, acquaintances, and members of my family who have asked so many times about this project can be told that I have finally published. Only the passage of time will determine if what I've written will make a difference, if only to a few.

This book is dedicated to the three most important women in

my life. My wife, Barbara, has been a constant source of support and encouragement, provided in a manner that I will characterize as gentle prodding but not nagging. My two daughters, Shannon and Shaun, have been aware of the project but never openly expressed any doubt about my ability or willingness to complete this book, although there must have been times when they asked themselves, "What's taking Dad so long to finish it?"

I also want to recognize and express my appreciation to a long-time friend and former investment broker, Bob Sawyer. We often visited with each other several times each weak. Over a period of several decades we discussed stocks, companies and investment philosophies (and sometimes politics). He, more than anyone else I've know, consistently stressed the virtues of looking for, analyzing, and investing in common stocks that are out-of-favor.

Finally, I want to thank everyone who comes into contact with this book. Your willingness to read all of the chapters or even browse through a few is a compliment to me and will provide a lasting feeling of accomplishment. If all that you remember is to concentrate your investments in a few good companies, I will have accomplished an important goal.

Richard L. Gunderson
Scottsdale, Arizona
March, 2012

INTRODUCTION
Common Stock Investing Today

Writing a book, especially for the first time, is a grueling task for many authors. But if the journey of putting words on paper begins with a clear understanding of the audience being targeted and the fundamental purpose of the book, the author can minimize some of the hard work and frustration. If an author has a clear idea regarding desired outcomes, he or she can enhance efforts to provide value to the reader.

I wrote *A Few Good Eggs in One Basket* for the individual investor as opposed to the institutional investor. The audience might also include individuals who are members of investment clubs. Investment professionals dealing primarily with individuals might also find some of the ideas useful in shaping an investment philosophy for clients whose views, temperaments, and objectives are compatible with the themes developed in this book.

I assume that the reader has some basic understanding of finance, accounting, and business; however, every attempt has been made to write in terms that can be understood without a lot of research. There may be times when the reader will need to consult business or financial reference material; however, an effort has been made to identify potential sources of information when a more complete understanding of a principle or concept might prove helpful in driving home a point.

I have targeted individual investors for a number of reasons. This group is as interested as any in achieving gains and avoiding losses. Individual investors are motivated to learn and understand. Those who are serious about investing a portion of their assets in common stocks are interested in acquiring or developing a better understanding of tools and concepts capable of sharpening their decision-making skills and improving investment performance. It is also likely that individual investors are in a better position to live with a philosophy that may not deliver above-average results every single quarter. However, the luxury of not having to strive for consistently good short-term performance represents a potential advantage the individual investor has over the professional money manager.

Investing in common stocks has been an interest and avocation of mine for over forty years. The experiences of investing have been rewarding in both a financial and emotional sense. The investment scene has changed considerably since the early 1960s. The price level of stocks has increased over tenfold in forty years, and the institutionalization of the market has been a major development. Many stocks have been extremely good investments, providing gains over this time period far in excess of the popular stock market averages. At the same time, other stock investments have been disappointing, producing returns less than that available on savings accounts. And most investors can point to at least one stock investment for which the return was negative.

Professional investors—investment analysts and portfolio managers—dominate the investment scene today. These professionals closely follow and quickly interpret the day-to-day and week-to-week developments of the companies and stocks in which they have an interest. Investment committees, supervisors, peers, and clients monitor their investment performance. The evaluation timeframe used for measuring performance is often very short. Monthly performance figures for portfolio managers are the norm, and annual, if not quarterly, formal performance reviews have become an accepted practice of fiduciary responsibility.

Preoccupation with short-term investment performance is excessive in the opinion of some people, a point of view I happen to share. News about a company or the stock market causes many investors to take action within minutes following the announcement. Modern communication technology makes it possible for investors anywhere in the world to evaluate almost simultaneously the implications of new developments in a given company. With this instant access to information and its scrutiny by trained and highly knowledgeable professionals, markets are becoming increasingly more efficient. Efficiency also means volatility.

Paradoxically, the dramatic changes that have taken place in capital markets over the past three decades have created opportunities for individual investors to achieve above-average returns relative to the market. Institutionalization of the investment process has produced a herd instinct that tends to generate overreaction to financial and economic news. This overreaction to negative developments creates potential opportunities for the well-informed and disciplined individual investor. However, the harsh reality is that capitalizing on the opportunities being created requires a contrarian mind-set—a willingness to defy conventional wisdom and popular opinion—along with a healthy dose of the courage and patience that are necessary to ride through the period of uncertainty with some confidence. This approach, however, does not require compromising investment quality. Since capital markets typically don't like uncertainty, it is possible for investors to buy quality at a lower price in exchange for greater uncertainty regarding investment performance in the future.

The practice of closely monitoring the performance of today's investment professionals has as one of its consequences a reluctance to buy out-of-favor stocks when the timeframe for price recovery is unknown. On the other hand, individual investors have available to them the luxury of not having to meet short-term performance objectives and, therefore, are able to take on the risk of uncertainty in return for investing in investment-quality stocks that have become available at a more attractive price than might have been the case only a few weeks earlier.

The market likes certainty and is willing to pay for it. Individual investors would do well to prioritize buying investment-quality stocks at attractive prices. That is most likely to occur following negative news or the release of information that clouds the near-term outlook or creates pessimism regarding future growth and profitability. Buying at a time of uncertainty places a premium on having a good understanding of the fundamentals of the company being considered for investment.

In summary, the current environment relating to capital markets and, in particular, common stocks, along with the vast amount of information available to anyone who's interested in mining it, represents an unprecedented opportunity for the individual investor to achieve respectable long-term returns. The challenge is to identify the stocks of good companies available at "cheap" prices and have the courage of one's convictions to own only a few of the issues that may be candidates for purchase at a given point in time. Information is plentiful, but discipline, good judgment, and patience are harder to come by. It is my hope and expectation that this book will enable individual investors to sharpen their skills, realize above-average investment returns, and experience even greater fulfillment in common stock investing.

Richard L. Gunderson, CFA

CHAPTER ONE

The Need for a Framework

Every common stock investor, institutional or individual, large or small, is faced with decisions about what, when, and how much to buy or sell of a security. These questions and many others require analysis and answers before sound decisions can be made. Managing investments, specifically common stocks, is a multifaceted decision-making process. Managing a common stock portfolio can be compared to managing a business. Business managers are confronted with choices and the need to make decisions, too. What markets should be served, what products should be offered, and what distribution channels should be used are but a few of the critical questions to answer. The quality of decisions made in a business has a great deal to do with the success of the enterprise. Consider the potential impact of a company's product development program. The company continuously makes decisions regarding what products to develop and which ones to abandon. There will always be uncertainty involving any decision about a new product, but the company can improve the odds of making the best decision by using an effective decision-making framework. Likewise, investment success is in large measure determined by the quality of decisions made regarding stock selection.

Just as there are many approaches to managing a business, there are many investment styles that can be used by an individual in managing a stock portfolio. Some people have been successful using a growth philosophy. Others have experienced excellent results using the value-investment philosophy. However, regardless of style, it appears that a critical element for continued success is the consistent application of a coherent framework and decision-making criteria. Developing the framework is important, but of equal, if not greater, importance is using it. Numerous studies have shown that novices as well as professionals make more accurate judgments when they follow systematic rules then when they rely on their intuition alone. Most investors share a common tendency to succumb to the emotional side of investing. A framework helps to keep emotions in check. With the information explosion, a systematic and disciplined approach is critical in order to efficiently and effectively sort through mountains of data and text and then make a sound decision.

Many investment-decision frameworks have proven to be successful over time, and several stand out as having stood the test of time measured in a period of many years or even decades. With all of the attention given to Warren Buffett—in the press or in books written by others about him and his successful style of investing—his has become a household name, and his accomplishments are legendary. There is no doubt that much of Buffett's success can be attributed to his disciplined approach to investing. He has a framework that evolved over time but seems to have remained stable in recent years. Buffett's framework—somewhat simplified—is based on the idea of buying stocks from a business point of view (as if you were going to own the entire corporation) in companies exhibiting these characteristics: predictable earnings; excellent business economics; a consumer monopoly; a high return on equity; and good management. Additionally, Buffett will purchase stock only when the price meets his rate-of-return objectives. Finally, he buys stock for the long term and assumes the stock will never be sold.

Peter Lynch, the professional money manager who established a great reputation during the years he managed Fidelity's Magellan Fund, had his unique framework. He looked for simple businesses that operated in slow-growing industries; were not followed by analysts or owned by institutions; had niches; offered products that people had to buy; and were users rather than sellers of technology.

The name Philip Fisher may not be familiar to many investors; however, during his long and active life as a professional investor he established a reputation among his peers that was second to none. Fisher began his career as an investment advisor in 1931, and went public in 1958 with his framework, "Fifteen Points to Look for in a Common Stock." The underlying themes of that framework include investing in companies with sustainable growth, high profitability, and a strong competitive advantage that are managed by individuals exhibiting unusual candor and high integrity. Like Warren Buffett, Fisher believed in limiting his investments to a few companies at a given point in time.

Some investors' frameworks are based simply on buying the shares of companies that are household names—companies whose products and services are valued, used, or consumed and considered to be of top quality by the investor. Many of these investors have purchased and held the shares of Procter and Gamble, Kimberly-Clark, McDonald's, General Mills, and Coca-Cola, to name a few, for years and even decades. This simple and straightforward framework has also proven to be very successful.

Consistent application of a framework will not always be comfortable, however. Independent thinking, courage, discipline, and patience are required. Adherence to a framework will not always be emotionally satisfying; at times it may even be boring. However, many investors have been successful because of their willingness to stay the course with their philosophies, avoiding the temptation to follow the crowd or get caught up in the most recent investment fad. Successful investing is all about achieving superior long-term investment returns, regardless of style or methodology.

This book offers a framework for the selection and management of common stocks in an individual portfolio. It is but one of many approaches and may not work equally well for everyone. But I can say on the basis of observation and personal experience, a well-constructed and consistently applied framework has the potential to deliver above-average returns, and consistency may be the most important factor.

I find a two-part framework to be useful. The first part relates to a broad investment philosophy that reflects how to view the dynamics of equity markets and, therefore, shapes one's thinking about an individual stock. The second part of the framework deals with stock selection—the specific attributes of a company and its common stock that should be evaluated and compared to established criteria and standards. This two-part framework governs my approach to investing and the contents of this book.

An Overarching Investment Philosophy

- Over the long term, US equity markets are efficient, and stock prices ultimately respond to the level of earnings, dividends, and interest rates. In the short term, stock prices react to new information and expectations—many times to extremes—resulting in volatility and price levels above or below intrinsic value.

- Reversion to the mean is an enduring phenomenon in equity markets and provides opportunities to purchase stocks at prices that will eventually prove to be attractive, thus providing an opportunity for enhancing long-term investment returns.

- It is unlikely that a highly diversified portfolio of investment-grade stocks will outperform an index fund over a period of many years.

- While concentration (owning only a few stocks at any given time) will increase the volatility of a portfolio, it is the best way to achieve above-average returns. Concentration should result in better and more consistently rewarding stock selection and forces an investor to own only those issues considered to possess the best risk/reward relationships.

- Attempting to time the purchase of an individual stock based on the level of the overall stock market is an exercise in futility.

- At any given point in time and in any market, there are stocks available at attractive prices. The challenge is to find them.

- High turnover is usually the enemy of above-average, long-term investment returns due to the impact of transaction costs and taxes on realized gains.

- Almost without exception, an undervalued stock involves lack of visibility and confidence regarding the trend of earnings and/or revenues, especially relating to the near-term outlook. Most investors inherently dislike uncertainty.

- When to sell an individual stock is the most difficult and uncertain aspect of the investment process. A decision to sell should be based on the price of a stock relative to its intrinsic value and longer-term outlook rather than on anticipated near-term price movements.

- Patience is a critically important attribute of successful investors. It is difficult to predict when an undervalued stock will return to or exceed its intrinsic value.

Framework for Stock Selection

The following constitute the remaining elements of the framework and relate specifically to stock analysis and stock selection:

1. **Is the stock of the company being considered out of favor or undiscovered, and does it appear to be undervalued?**

   The underlying premise of this framework is that undervalued stocks, properly selected, will produce investment returns superior to market averages. It is likely that stocks of companies temporarily out of favor (or for whatever reason ignored by investors) may be undervalued and could represent an attractive risk/gain opportunity.

2. **Does the potential exist for a significant gain?**

   Invest only when there is an opportunity for a significant long-term gain. As a guideline look for stocks with the potential for a 25 to 30 percent annualized gain over a period of several years.

3. **Is the company effectively led and well managed?**

   Effective leadership is a key determinant in the long-term success of a company. To be well managed, a company must attract and retain employees who possess competence and exhibit good judgment, dedication, and integrity. Outstanding people represent a real competitive advantage; mediocre talent may result in poor implementation of even the best strategy.

4. **What is unique about the company?**

   A company with unique qualities may have a competitive edge and may be accorded a premium valuation by investors.

5. **Is there a clear, focused, and viable strategy that can be implemented?**

   The management of the company must have a game plan that is right for the times, well understood, supported by the organization, and capable of being implemented with resources that exist or can be acquired. The strategy should reflect a focus on the customer and a commitment to continuous improvement in all phases of the business.

6. **Does the company have open-ended opportunities to pursue?**

   Open-ended opportunities represent the potential for above-average growth, which can lead to a higher valuation of earnings by investors. Growth can be more readily sustained and earnings prospects are more predictable if sales to customers are frequent and of a recurring nature.

7. **Is the company financially viable and capable of financing its growth?**

   Avoid situations in which the company has an exceptionally weak balance sheet or may be unable to fund its debt service. Financial strength and staying power are essential to capitalizing on significant opportunities, dealing with adversity, and resolving problems. The best of all worlds is finding the undervalued stock of a company with little or no debt and significant cash flow.

8. **Does the company have the potential to earn an above-average return on equity?**

   An above-average return on equity (ROE) is critical to financing the growth of the company without significant dilution of earnings. Of the factors determining ROE, profit margins are among the most critical. While imperfect, ROE is a useful and legitimate measure of management performance.

9. **To what extent does management have an ownership stake in the company?**

   A significant ownership position by members of management and other insiders represents a visible alignment of interests with those of investors. Absence of meaningful stock ownership or a significant reduction in insider holdings immediately before or after making a purchase should be a cause for concern.

The elements of this framework will be discussed in greater detail throughout the book, but they can be summarized as follows: select companies that are well managed and financially strong and have a unique position in their markets; make your purchase of a stock when it is out of favor and undervalued; own no more than five to ten issues at a given point in time; sell an existing holding only when you find another stock that offers superior long-term value or if you have made a mistake in buying an existing holding; and be patient, disciplined, and willing to defy conventional wisdom. This framework resulted in the title of this book, *A Few Good Eggs in One Basket*.

My hope and expectation is that the proposed framework will be useful to individual investors who have the interest and desire to build their net worth over a period of time through selecting and owning individual stocks. While I've not always applied the framework consistently in my own situation, my mistakes and disappointments have typically been the result of an overly liberal interpretation of the framework or outright violation of one or more of its elements.

CHAPTER TWO

Out of Favor and Undervalued

believe that the odds of achieving above-average investment returns are improved by buying (or selling) stocks at a point in time when it is contrary to what is being done by a majority of other investors. I have heard the term *leaning into the wind* used to describe this approach to stock investing. Investors generally are willing to pay a premium for high earnings visibility, but when uncertainty or disappointment begins to dominate investor thinking, stock prices are negatively affected, especially for those companies that may be overvalued. The speed with which new information becomes widely known and the hunger for "good" performance on the part of professional money managers can, and often does, cause a change in the stock price of a particular company over a very short period of time—days or, in many cases, hours. These sudden swings in valuation are referred to as volatility. Higher risk is associated with higher volatility; however, it can also be viewed as an indicator of opportunity, especially for the investor who has the luxury of buying a stock and not having to worry about relative or absolute performance in the short run.

Having the freedom to act in a contrary manner and buy a stock when the outlook is uncertain and the price is below its assumed fair or intrinsic value represents a unique opportunity for the individual investor. Assuming the out-of-favor or undiscovered status is temporary, being willing to buy when others are not offers the potential benefit of higher returns and reduced risk since the lower price presumably is discounting the prevailing uncertainty. However, the assumption regarding the temporary nature of being out of favor should not be taken lightly. There are what some investors refer to as "value traps." If a stock has declined significantly, there is always a reason for it, and the circumstances causing the change in price of the stock must be evaluated. It is not uncommon for a stock to decline and remain at a lower level for a period of several quarters or even years because the business fundamentals of the company have changed.

Historical Record for Out-of-Favor Stocks

Over a decade ago a very thought-provoking study was published providing evidence that buying out-of-favor stocks results in above-average returns.[1] The study demonstrated that during the period between 1968 and 1990 out-of-favor stocks outperformed so-called glamour issues by more than 10 percent per year. The authors offered a number of explanations for their findings including that (a) there appears to be a systematic pattern on the part of both individual and institutional investors to overestimate the future growth rates of glamour stocks by placing excessive weight on recent history, despite the fact that future growth rates are mean reverting; (b) there's a tendency for investors to buy or recommend so-called good companies with steady earnings and dividend growth irrespective of price; and (c) many investors have timeframes shorter than what is required for out-of-favor investments to pay off. It's likely, therefore, that a majority of investors have a bias for quality and predictability owing to the desire for peace of mind and to act prudently.

The possibility exists, of course, that equity market dynamics have changed since 1994. However, a more recent study comparing out-of-favor stocks to market stars during the period from 1975 to 2004 confirms the findings of Lakonishok, Shleifer, and Vishny.[2] In fact the more recent study indicates that out-of-favor stocks outperformed the stars by an even greater margin than the 1994 study—nearly 20 percent annually. Once again an interpretation of the research results attributed the performance differential to overly optimistic projections of future growth and what some economists call agency issues: investment styles, concerns about excessive deviations from benchmarks, and institutional practices.

And now for the sixty-four-dollar question: Will the positive performance differential of out-of-favor stocks continue well into the future? Despite the persistence of this differential over many decades, the possibility exists that due to the forces of computerized trading, the dominating influence of hedge funds, growth in the use of derivatives, and awareness of arbitrage opportunities, the performance differential could narrow or even vanish. However, my interpretation of these and other factors leads me to believe the performance gap will continue. These factors include (a) the dislike investors have for uncertainty, and the fact that, when a perception suddenly emerges that a company is faced with a new uncertainty, whether in the short or long term, sellers will outnumber buyers and the price of the stock will decline and it may become out of favor; (b) that hedge funds will typically sell a stock short in the face of uncertainty, causing a precipitous and oftentimes excessive price decline; and (c) that investors' focus on short-term performance appears to be an enduring phenomenon, and that changing would represent a major challenge to the theory of efficient markets. In summary, my own conclusion is that the positive performance differential of out-of-favor stocks will continue—most likely by a significant margin.

If my assumptions are wrong, the risk is that out-of-favor stocks will do no better or worse than the stars. My rationale for that statement is that the principle of reversion to the mean would cause the performance differential to vanish.

Crowd Psychology and Stock Prices

There is evidence dating back hundreds of years that prices are influenced by crowd psychology. One of the most famous examples involves the tulip mania in the Netherlands during the seventeenth century. The country had become a center for the development of new tulip varieties. Professional growers and wealthy individuals who liked flowers created a market for tulips. By 1636 the rapid price increases for the bulbs, especially those considered to be rare varieties, attracted speculators. In February 1637, prices for some tulips increased twenty-five-fold, but shortly thereafter prices collapsed, in some cases by more than 90 percent.

Netscape Communication, Inc., the pioneer in the development and introduction of the web browser, is a 1990s example of stock price mania. This company went public in August of 1995. The offering price was twenty-eight dollars per share, which represented a total market value for the company of $2.5 billion. At the time of the offering Netscape had reported trailing twelve-month revenues of about $22 million, but no profit. The initial offering price of the stock was, therefore, more than one hundred times revenues. At about that same time the market value of General Motors was about one-fourth the annual revenues of the company reported for 1995. The price of Netscape eventually climbed from twenty-eight dollars to an all-time high of eighty dollars prior to the end of 1995, at which time the total market value of the company exceeded $7 billion. Less than three years later the price of Netscape common stock had declined to less than fifteen dollars per share, even though revenues had increased more than twentyfold since the time of the offering.

The impact of crowd psychology should not be a surprise since a change in consensus regarding the outlook for a company and what it's worth causes a shift in the supply/demand relationship for its shares. What is interesting, however, is contemplating what influences a change in the consensus. In his book *The Art of Contrary Thinking*, Humphrey Neill describes the natural tendency of crowds to follow what they assume to be the action of the opinion leader; if an idea attracts a few people, it is likely to attract a wider following. Neill goes on to state that a crowd does not think; it acts on impulses and is influenced by feelings and sentiment. This phenomenon applies to the stock market where the crowd (investors and speculators) typically remains indifferent when prices are low or stable. The public seems to be attracted by activity and price movement, especially rising prices. Crowd psychology is also at work in the arena occupied by professional investors; however, these investors seem to be attracted by price movements in either direction. Neill postulates that an important characteristic of a crowd is the susceptibility to a suggestion, which can be contagious, and it is the power of suggestion that motivates their actions. The crowd phenomenon also helps explain why the stock price of a given company typically reflects a wide trading range over the course of a year. New information is shared and evaluated by one or more opinion leaders. The more credible the source, the more likely investors (the crowd) are to accept the suggestion, leading to the emergence of a different consensus and a shift in the price of the stock. In the case of Netscape, the company was backed by one of the most successful venture capital firms in the country. Additionally, a very prestigious investment banker managed the initial public offering. These two realities set the stage for the investing public to follow the lead of highly credible opinion leaders.

In today's environment one can witness a 15 to 20 percent change in the price of a stock overnight, even though the opinion leader may have overreacted to or reached an incorrect conclusion about the fundamentals of the company. Stock prices are continuously being impacted by feelings and sentiment—sometimes to an extreme.

Regression to the Mean

A phenomenon involving the market for common stocks (as well as many other areas) that is fascinating to contemplate involves the notion that prices tend to fluctuate around a trend line, and there are forces that, over time, drive prices to a central tendency. We have often heard the statement that what goes up must come down; and I would add, what goes down may go up at some point, especially if the decline is precipitous.

The principle of regression to the mean is a statistical phenomenon discovered by Sir Francis Galton, an Englishman, over one hundred years ago. In simple terms the principle is similar to several everyday expressions such as "the law of averages" and "things will even out." A value investor by the name of David Dreman wrote about this subject in the late 1970s as it relates to stock prices.[3] He emphasized that extreme returns in stock prices, either positive or negative, are unlikely to persist, the greater probability being that succeeding patterns will tend to fall in line with historical norms. He also reminded us that many investors overlook this principle because of their preoccupation with short-term trends in stock prices. More recently, an economist and author by the name of Ben Stein described regression to the mean as the "stretchy rubber band" that eventually pulls back stock prices to a more normal relationship.[4]

Regression to the mean is not a concept that's accepted intuitively. However, it occurs in many situations that we can relate to. For example, a running back in the NFL might establish in a given season a record of 4.3 yards per carry. This represents an average computed by dividing total net year's gains for the season by the number of carries. However, the statistic is the result of some carries of a yard or two and others involving twenty or thirty yards and more. Not every play is designed to produce a touchdown, and many plays fall short of expectations for reasons of poor offensive execution or excellent defense. But over time a game plan will produce short gains as well as long gains, and over time the yards per carry will average out.

And so it is with stock prices. Over a period of decades, stock prices of large companies have averaged a total return of about 10 percent annually; however that statistic includes a year with a positive return exceeding 50 percent (1954) and a negative return in excess of 40 percent (1931). As in football, where it is difficult to predict which play will produce the long gain, it is equally difficult to forecast which year stock market returns will be significantly higher or lower than the long-term average. However, over time, returns will migrate to a long-term trend. Individual stock prices will show significant fluctuations over the course of a year; but, over time, the rate of appreciation in the price of a stock will follow the trend of earnings per share.

Therefore, if the price of a given stock experiences a sharp decline, and the reasons for the decline are transitory, the price should eventually rebound so that the total investment return over time mirrors the financial performance of the company. It is the principle of regression to the mean that should provide investors with the rationale and courage to take advantage of market corrections and declines in the price of an individual security. A stock can become overpriced as well, and the same principle of regression to the mean will result in a correction—sometimes a major decline.

Out-of-Favor Indicators

At this point it is appropriate to ask how an investor determines that a stock is out of favor. The most visible indicator is a significant decline in price from a recent high. A rule of thumb for me is a decline of 50 percent or more from the fifty-two-week high. While it is acknowledged that the fifty-two-week high may have occurred as a result of investor euphoria or a stock very popular for a time with momentum investors, a significant decline for any reason usually causes investors to stay on the sidelines for a while and look for reasons why fundamentals have changed. A significant decline coupled with a change in the outlook for the growth rate and profitability of a company usually generates even stronger negative feelings on the part of investors.

Another indicator is the profile of ratings provided by analysts who follow a company. The rating profile is available from a number of sources; however, I find the First Call Earnings Valuation Report to be both current and sufficiently complete to make a judgment about the attitude of analysts following a company. If most or all of the analysts following a stock have a neutral or sell rating, one can assign the stock to the out-of-favor category. There are situations where a stock may have peaked two or three years earlier and the price has remained stable at a level considerably below an earlier high. The inability of a stock to resume an upward price trend is another indication of its being out of favor. Although extremely rare, a stock followed by many analysts, all of whom have rated the stock as a sell, would be the most obvious example of being out of favor. Given the reluctance of many analysts to assign a sell rating to a stock, a neutral or underperform rating, if in the majority, reflects an out-of-favor status.

Why Stocks Fall Out of Favor

Investors should assume that a stock is out of favor for a reason. The challenge, therefore, is to determine if the reasons are valid and the extent to which those reasons reflect a fundamental change in the future and fortunes of the company. The reasons may involve internal problems such as quality or reliability of a major product line. Prospects for lower sales and earnings than had been anticipated by investors frequently result in disfavor as will a significant operating loss. The expiration of patent protection for a key product with nothing on the horizon to fill the gap will result in investor disenchantment. The departure of a CEO or CFO introduces uncertainty and, depending on circumstances, could result in a significant drop in the company's stock price.

External factors frequently lead to a change in investor attitude. Price competition, new and better products by peer companies, threats of new legislation, or intervention by government can also result in causing a company or even an industry to slip into the out-of-favor camp.

The more significant the threat and the longer its perceived duration, the greater the impact on the stock price, particularly if the price of the stock at the time of discovery is above its fair value.

It is quite obvious, therefore, that assessing the severity and duration of the problem is the major challenge in determining whether or not out-of-favor status translates to a buying opportunity. It is also important to assess the staying power of the company, especially in terms of the strength of its balance sheet and liquidity. Severe problems that require several quarters or years to rectify, together with a weak balance sheet, represent the classic characteristics of a value trap. Investors who choose to own a limited number of stocks should avoid true value traps; companies so categorized are difficult to value and the timing and degree of recovery are highly uncertain. In today's rapidly changing and highly competitive environment, a company that stumbles in a significant way not only suffers a penalty in terms of the time and resources required to fix the problem, but is also in the position of losing competitive advantage, thereby being even more vulnerable to loss of both customer loyalty and investor confidence.

The risk that an out-of-favor stock is representative of a company with an unattractive future is very real. "Cheap" stocks do not necessarily equate to good value; they may remain cheap for many years.

Value Trap versus Value Stock

When an individual investor follows the path of portfolio concentration, he or she *must* be very selective in choosing what stocks to purchase. While owning only a few names affords the investor the opportunity to be selective, it also requires avoiding stocks for which the price might move sideways for years or, worse yet, continue to decline significantly following purchase. Within that context it's imperative to minimize, if not eliminate, the potential for buying a stock that appears undervalued but in fact represents partial ownership of a company in serious trouble with limited or no opportunity for positive returns. This leads us to a question: how should an investor go about identifying legitimate value and avoid the value trap?

Investors frequently define value stocks as those with a low price-earnings ratio or low ratio of price to book value. I have chosen to use the term *value* in relationship to a stock that sells at a significant discount to intrinsic value, however that might be calculated. My personal experience has led me to conclude that intrinsic value at a given point in time is a function of a company's earning power, the future growth of earnings, and many other factors that are continuously changing in the eyes of investors but that in reality can be considered relatively stable in the short run.

The first step in the stock selection process is identifying value candidates—stocks that on the surface appear to be selling at a discount to fair value. Identification normally will involve designing a screen or establishing criteria to be used in compiling a list of stocks that appear to be suitable candidates for purchase. The criteria should include stocks whose prices have experienced a significant decline within the past twelve months and show a relationship between price and earning power that is attractive relative to the market, its peer group, or a list of stocks with similar characteristics. The price-earnings ratio is one example of such a measure. I have observed that many out-of-favor stocks experience (and eventually report) a decline in earnings. Depressed earnings can result in an inflated price-earnings ratio, and when that situation occurs I find it appropriate to use the price-to-sales ratio as a way of comparing valuation levels. There are also tools available that can be used to quickly measure fair value on a discounted cash flow basis, representing yet another approach to identifying candidates—comparing current price to computed value.

After identifying a stock that appears to be undervalued, an important next step is determining the major reasons why. Without undertaking the more comprehensive analysis that must ultimately be done, I propose examining the company within the context of five parameters (described in greater detail in chapter four): competitive advantage; open-ended opportunities; corporate health; financial vitality; and earnings continuity. If the company rates below average on all of those five parameters and if there appears to be little or no chance the situation will improve, stop your work and move on to another idea. Remember, a concentrated portfolio demands that you look for outstanding investment opportunities and not be satisfied with mediocrity.

One of the more interesting approaches to identifying stocks that are both out of favor and undervalued was revealed in *The Little Book That Beats the Market* by Joel Greenblatt, the founder and managing partner of Gotham Capital.[5] The author refers to his approach as the Magic Formula, and it is based on ranking companies on the basis of two factors: return on capital and earnings yield. Return on capital is measured by calculating the ratio of pretax operating earnings (EBIT) to tangible capital employed (net working capital + net fixed assets); earnings yield is measured by calculating the ratio of pretax operating earnings (EBIT) to enterprise value (market value of equity + interest-bearing debt). The Magic Formula, when applied to a universe of stocks, produces ratios that can be ranked. The companies that have both a high earnings yield and a high return on capital are the ones given the highest rating. As the author states, the formula makes it possible to identify "above average companies at below average prices." The updated list can be viewed weekly by going to the website currently being maintained by Greenblatt (www.magicformula.com). I have refined this approach by ranking the stocks on the list on the basis of the earnings yield and then determining the mean of the fifty-two-week high and fifty-two-week low and calculating the potential increase in price were the stock to move from its current level to the fifty-two-week mean. Another list is generated by ranking the percentage gain to the mean from high to low. The Magic Formula approach limits the initial list to one hundred, with the critical filter being the size of market cap being considered. The Magic Formula makes it possible for an individual investor to quickly generate a list of common stocks that can be analyzed in depth, and the refinement I have developed is capable of further reducing the size of the list. The selection criteria of high returns reduces the risk of falling prey to value traps, and calculating the potential gain to the mean represents another way to identify stocks that are out of favor to varying degrees (stocks with the highest gain potential have experienced the most significant percentage decline in the past twelve months).

Undiscovered Stocks

Although finding stocks that have been ignored by investors is becoming increasingly rare, on occasion they do appear on the scene. And sometimes their discovery represents the best of both worlds: companies with strong fundamentals and clean balance sheets that are available at a significant discount to the intrinsic value of the stock. My own experience involves finding small-cap companies for which coverage by brokerage house analysts has been very limited or nonexistent. There are also companies whose stocks may have been out of favor for many years for a variety of legitimate reasons, but for whom time and resources have rectified the problems although investors have not recognized the progress that's been made.

Using screening tools is an effective way of identifying stocks that are being ignored by investors. The Fidelity website provides a screening program for its customers that can be useful in identifying stocks meeting selected criteria. A screen has been developed for identifying stocks that have low institutional investor ownership—another indicator of undiscovered stocks. At the time I ran this screen over 300 issues were identified, and roughly 5 percent of the stocks showed zero institutional ownership. The website money.msn.com has a number of screens appropriate for value investors, including ready-made screens that identify fifty-two-week or five-year lows, contrarian ideas, and stocks that have been beaten down but have the potential to bounce back. While screens cannot replace human judgment, their availability online makes it possible for an individual investor to quickly identify a group of stocks meeting specific criteria, which, in turn, allows one to spend more time comprehensively analyzing which stocks are best suited for the portfolio.

Chapter Summary

- In the short term, stock prices fluctuate to a much greater degree than the variation in underlying fundamentals of the company.

- Crowd psychology contributes to price volatility as do legitimate changes in investor sentiment and expectations.

- Extreme returns in stock prices are unlikely to persist. The phenomenon of regression to the mean is like a rubber band that eventually pulls stock prices back to more normal relationships.

- A stock falls out of favor because of major uncertainties or threats. The resulting price decline presents a challenge to the enterprising investor, who is faced with the task of assessing the severity and duration of the problem and then determining whether or not the out-of-favor status translates to a buying opportunity.

- Individual investors will benefit from a tool kit that makes it possible to improve the odds of identifying stocks of above-average companies that can be bought at below-average prices.

CHAPTER THREE
Significant Uniqueness

In consulting the dictionary we discover the earliest meanings of the word *unique*, first introduced into the English language around 1600, were "single" and "having no equal." By the mid-nineteenth century the word had developed a broader meaning: "not typical, unusual." It is my intention to use the term to convey something between "having no equal" and "unusual," specifically with regard to characteristics or attributes of a company that represent a competitive advantage in the marketplace.

My first job following graduate school was with the St. Paul Fire and Marine Insurance Company (later renamed the St. Paul Companies), where for my first thirteen of twenty-four years with the organization I analyzed stocks and bonds, and managed investment portfolios. One of the unique attributes of St. Paul was its distinction of being the company with the oldest corporate charter (founded in 1853) in the state of Minnesota. Although unique (having no equal), the distinction had no significance with respect to competitive advantage. I cannot recall ever hearing about recruiting a new agent or winning a new customer because of the corporate charter; that distinction had no relevance in the marketplace.[6]

From an investment point of view, identifying and evaluating the uniqueness of a company is important for two reasons: (1) when uniqueness relates to establishing and maintaining a strong competitive position it can be a powerful and sustaining driver of profitability and revenue growth; (2) of lesser importance, if perceived as an unusual and enduring strength, uniqueness can create a scarcity value for the stock and positively impact valuation. Within this context it seems useful to list the more obvious examples of uniqueness that might be present in a given company:

- market leadership

- position as lowest cost producer

- effective distribution system

- highly productive research and development effort

- strong culture of innovation

- strong brand image and high level of customer awareness

- strong patent position

- outstanding reputation for quality and reliability

- low-cost or high-quality natural resources

- one-of-a kind databases with proprietary content

- core competencies involving know-how, experience, and expertise

- product lines with very high switching costs

- large and loyal customer base

Although information with regard to each of these examples may not be readily available, many investors would be surprised about what they could glean from the Form 10-K or annual report of a company.

In some instances investors have a sense of where a company stands out. For example, few would argue about Microsoft's strong brand, high level of consumer awareness, and large customer base; most investors (and competitors) are aware of the broad and strong patent portfolio of the 3M Company; and Intel is noted for uniqueness in technological know-how. No single company will be significantly unique in all of the areas listed above; however, careful evaluation will usually reveal one or more unique attributes that have contributed to its success. Absence of a significant uniqueness should be considered a red flag and a potential precursor to competitive mediocrity and lackluster stock performance.

There is also a less visible but equally profound type of uniqueness; it can best be described as a company whose operational activities are individually and collectively integrated with and highly supportive of the organization's strategy.[7] Uniqueness of this type has the following benefits with respect to competitive advantage:

- It is more difficult for a competitor to emulate an integrated system; therefore, a company in this position will have a more sustainable competitive advantage, particularly if the elements of the system and the integration process are continuously being improved.

- Assuming the strategy is right for the chosen market, the customer is the beneficiary of better value because of the alignment of product, service, and price. Customers who are satisfied will tell others, thereby assisting the company in increasing market share. Customers who consistently experience or perceive that they are receiving good value develop a strong loyalty, which in itself becomes a source of competitive advantage.

- While significant uniqueness does not eliminate the need for efficiency, it represents a way of competing more on the basis of value rather than price.

- Combining operational and strategic integration with other significantly unique attributes of a company offers the best opportunity for above-average profit margins and investment returns.

I have never invested in an airline stock, and I'm not about to embark on a mission of advocacy at this point. However, it is useful to examine the financial performance and return to shareholders of an airline that is an example of the benefits of operational and strategic integration. Southwest Airlines is unique among the larger carriers. Its policies and practices with respect to choice and type of routes; use of one type of aircraft; baggage handling; boarding procedures; compensation of employees; schedule reliability; and no-frills approach have been tightly integrated with the strategy of low ticket prices. This approach has served Southwest extremely well during a period of industry turmoil and consolidation. Shareholders have prospered as well, both in absolute terms and relative to shareholders in the stocks of competing airlines. Southwest's approach to integration and focus has been extremely difficult to replicate by the larger carriers, though some have tried without much success. Some of the newer carriers such as Jet Blue have learned from Southwest's experience.

In today's fast-moving and highly competitive environment, two forms of uniqueness deserve special mention: core competencies and a strong culture of innovation. I will discuss these two attributes and several others in greater detail below. Although uniqueness or lack thereof may be difficult for the individual investor to ascertain, its impact on long-term financial results and shareholder value is real. In that respect, an examination of the company's track record may be the most reliable indicator of uniqueness. Consistently high returns on capital, above-average profit margins, and a stock price selling at a significant premium to book value all point to the existence of unique attributes.

Core Competencies

It can be argued that competition between firms is as much a function of unique capabilities or competencies as it is of market position. In the book *Competing for the Future*, Gary Hamel and C. K. Prahalad advocate that the senior management of a company must focus attention on those competencies that lie at the center of long-term competitive success, referred to as core competencies.[8] The authors postulate that a core competency must meet three tests:

- Customer value: Core competencies are the skills that enable a company to deliver an important customer benefit. They must make a disproportionate contribution to customer-perceived value.

- Competitor differentiator: Core competencies must be competitively unique. That is, they must be substantially superior to similar competencies possessed by others.

- Extendibility: They must be applicable in new product areas. Even though a competency meets the test of customer value and competitive uniqueness, the authors state that it is not a *core* competency if there is no opportunity to apply it to new initiatives.

Core competencies are not assets; they are not factories, distribution channels, brands, or patents. However, the aptitude and skills associated with managing assets and functions can be regarded as core. Unique engineering, marketing, product design, and distribution skills are examples of core competencies, assuming they meet the test previously outlined. An individual investor should read published reports about a company being analyzed to determine if there are unique aptitudes and skills that set the company apart from the competition and will continue to do so in the future.

Core competencies require time to develop—years, not months—and are the by-product of commitment, experience, and activity. There's a learning curve that represents a potential barrier to a competitor. If, as a result of fully developing the right competencies, an organization becomes very good at what's important for business success, this creates a competitive advantage that has the potential to be sustainable for a meaningful period of time. However, core competence leadership may be diminished or even lost for a variety of reasons including underfunding, fragmentation of responsibility, and/or loss of organizational focus. Protecting core competencies requires diligence on the part of top management, whose responsibility it is to continuously reinforce awareness and their importance to the success of the enterprise.

A Strong Culture of Innovation

Over a period of several decades, much has been written about the importance of innovation. The legendary Peter Drucker wrote extensively about innovation and described it as the design and development of something new that will establish a new economic configuration out of the old, known, existing elements. It is the missing link between having a number of disconnected elements, each marginally effective, and an integrated system of great power.[9] In a lead article in the November 2006 issue of *Harvard Business Review*, author Rosabeth Moss Kanter describes the re-emergence of innovation as a high corporate priority and then recalls past attempts over the past twenty-five years involving grandiose plans that were followed by mediocre execution and poor results. She goes on to characterize the waves of enthusiasm for innovation, each involving the tension between protecting existing revenue streams and supporting new initiatives that companies thought might be critical to their future success.

Innovation has not only been the subject of business writers and academics for a long time, it's been successfully practiced for many decades as well. In his book *Built to Last*, Jim Collins discusses an interview with Bill Hewlett, one of the founders of Hewlett-Packard, who was asked to name a company that he greatly admired and would single out as a role model. Without hesitation he named 3M. Collins agreed with Hewlett and further stated that, if he had to bet his life on the success and adaptability of a single company over the next fifty to one hundred years, it would be 3M.[10] Business history strongly indicates that one of the early presidents of 3M, William McKnight, created the organizational climate that resulted in a strong and enduring culture of innovation. McKnight intuitively understood that encouraging individual initiative would lead to evolutionary progress; and he also understood that not every initiative would prove successful. Some of McKnight's memorable phrases, recorded during his tenure as CEO and quoted long after he retired, are below:

- "Listen to anyone with an original idea, no matter how absurd it might sound."

- "Encourage, don't nitpick. Let people run with an idea."

- "If you put fences around people, you get sheep. Give people the room they need."

- "Encourage experimental doodling."

- "Give it a try—and quick!"

These common-sense phrases—and, no doubt, many other statements made by other leaders at 3M—provided the framework and discipline for innovation that has led to thousands of new products (including but not limited to such blockbusters as Scotch tape and Post-it notes) and an enviable record of growth and profitability spanning more than seventy-five years.

While there may be general agreement about the need for and benefits of innovation, there is less of a consensus regarding how best to achieve meaningful innovation within a company. Certainly 3M's approach has worked, but in many other companies efforts have floundered. In the past, innovation was thought to be the responsibility of the corporate R&D (research and development) function. But many companies have learned that the R&D budget was increasing faster than the payoff. The management of Procter and Gamble (P&G) faced up to this dilemma following the appointment of A. G. Lafley as CEO. Lafley realized that creating organic growth of 5 percent per year for a company the size of P&G would require more than a developed-from-within approach to new products. He then challenged top management to reinvent the company's innovation business model, which ultimately resulted in the decision to actively develop external connections as a way of acquiring innovations from outside the company.[11] This approach was not designed to replace the internal development staff but rather to better leverage them. The results have been quite dramatic in that the company's innovation success rate has doubled; R&D productivity has increased by nearly 70 percent; and R&D investment as a percent of sales has declined. The management of P&G believe that their innovation model, referred to as "connect and develop," will become the dominant model for the twenty-first century, and that the more traditional approach (developing exclusively from within) is a path to diminishing returns. Lafley emphasized that the CEO of an organization must make the approach to innovation a top priority; and the related strategy should include a commitment to innovate based on ideas and resources from outside the organization.

In my research on the subject of innovation, I came across the results of a survey conducted in 2000 by the consulting arm of PricewaterhouseCoopers.[12] The executive summary of the published report begins with a crisp yet comprehensive definition of innovation: "the successful implementation of new ideas in any aspect of business." I consider those words to be both thought-provoking and reassuring since, on reflection, innovation is beneficial not only with respect to new products and services, but also in generating enhancements to existing product lines and improved distribution, service, processes, and procedures.

The results of the survey revealed that even though the management of most companies would like their organizations to be innovative, many fall far short of achieving the benefits. One startling conclusion of the report was that the top innovators can generate over 75 percent of their revenue from products and services not in existence five years earlier. For the poorest performers the corresponding number is 10 percent or less. These results by and large were independent of the market sector served by the company, and the top performers represent a diverse group in terms of both size and type of business. What separates the best innovators from the poorest was explained in the report by ten characteristics.[13] Trust was the number one differentiator, empowering individuals to communicate and implement change in order to convert ideas into reality. The top 20 percent in the survey turned their ideas into action using a well-defined idea management process that did the following:

- gathered ideas and knowledge from a wide range of customers, employees, suppliers, and other industries;

- allowed the information captured from the various sources to be shared and made freely accessible;

- actively encouraged diversity of viewpoints, talent, and expertise; and

- delayed the premature evaluation of anything new by giving managers considerable discretion to pursue new ideas without subjecting them to formal appraisals.

One of the major conclusions of the survey is that there are no magic bullets regarding successful innovation. What is critical is the need for making innovation a priority, starting with the board of directors and CEO. Company leaders must establish a climate and a process that encourages and rewards employees and other key constituency groups for identifying, trying, and implementing new ideas. Innovation is not rocket science, but it does require commitment, discipline, and perseverance.

One more point needs to be made about innovation. Most businessmen would acknowledge that in today's fast-moving, competitive environment the duration of most competitive advantages is shrinking. The success of a new product, service, or process soon becomes visible, and competitors respond. Sustainable competitive advantage, therefore, requires constant change in the product and service offerings and continuous improvement in the processes serving the customer. For a business to grow and prosper, maintaining the status quo is not an option. It is difficult for an individual investor to assess management's commitment to a successful program of innovation. However, consistent with the findings in the PWC survey, a clear indicator of both commitment and success is the percentage of revenues generated by products and services introduced within the past five years.[14]

Strong Brand Image and Customer Awareness

Nearly every company has a brand, and some have many. Brands are important because they can help persuade customers to purchase one product rather than another. In today's highly competitive environment, differentiation of products and services is difficult to achieve, let alone sustain. Therefore, a brand that is unique and strong represents power to gain and/or sustain market share. Strong brands have another advantage: they can command a price premium, thereby making it easier to achieve and maintain attractive profit margins.

In the late 1990s, Philip Kotler, then professor of marketing at the Kellogg School of Management, wrote and lectured extensively on the subject of brands.[15] He made the point that "the art of marketing is largely the act of brand building" and went on to state that when something is not a brand, it will probably viewed as a commodity, at which point price becomes the differentiator. When price is critical the only winner is the low-cost producer. Kotler also states that brands are strong when their name conveys positive attributes and benefits.

Brands are important in both consumer and commercial markets. A study conducted by principals in the McKinsey organization and published in the *McKinsey Quarterly* revealed that, in both consumer and business-to-business markets, brand was a key factor underlying the purchase decision. On average the brand was responsible for 18 percent of the total decision, although there was considerable variance between the highest (39 percent) and the lowest (3 percent) brand-importance rating.[16] The study also revealed prices of the strongest brands, on average, were 19 percent higher than those of the weakest brands.

Based on marketplace experience and observations made by acknowledged experts in the field of marketing, I have concluded that the stronger and more unique the brand, the better the odds that market share and above-average margins can be sustained or even increased. This assumption, if valid, should provide encouragement to investors who are considering the purchase of an out-of-favor company with a portfolio of products having a strong and positive brand identity with customers.

Reputation for Quality and Reliability

If, as stated by Kotler, a strong brand is intended to convey positive attributes and benefits, the products and services being offered must have a reputation for quality and reliability; they go hand in hand. Consumers and buyers vote with their feet and credit cards, and their loyalties can change quickly if they have a string of experiences that fall short of expectations. Equally important, a user of a product or service who is disappointed will tell others about it (I once read that a consumer having a bad experience will on average tell nineteen other people). Thus, a poor or declining reputation for quality has a compounding effect. Not only is the company vulnerable to losing one customer, but also many more.

Information and data providing insights about product quality and reliability is not always available or comparable, thereby making it difficult to determine where a company ranks on either a relative or absolute basis. However, there are instances in which judgments can be made on the basis of what isn't being discussed by management in their reports or news releases. If the management of a company has made quality and reliability a true priority, metrics will have been put in place to monitor results, and if the results are exceptionally good, they are likely to be highlighted in some way. There are situations in which management will be very clear and explicit regarding a commitment to continuous improvement or being a leader in quality. While there are pros and cons to instituting Six Sigma initiatives (the emphasis may be on cost reduction as opposed to quality improvement or enhanced features), evidence of such efforts is a tangible way for management to indicate its priorities. My own way of assessing management's intentions or actual performance in this regard is to look for statements in the annual report or 10-K on the subject of quality and reliability. In the absence of such statements, I assume there is nothing significantly unique on which to build a case for stock ownership, even though that is only one of many factors to be considered.

Market Leadership

Early in his tenure as CEO of General Electric, Jack Welch began insisting that the company's products lines be number one or two in the markets served. One might ask, "Why should that be so important?" Perhaps the simple answer is that market dominance has its advantages. However, bigger is not necessarily better. There is more to market leadership than share points.

In the mid-1960s a team from General Electric initiated and developed a project called Profit Impact of Market Strategy (PIMS), which revealed a positive correlation between profitability, product quality, and market. Although the benefits of market share as posited by PIMS have been challenged in recent years, those who believe in its validity remain in the majority. However, there is evidence that the importance of market share varies by industry: it is greater for fragmented industries and infrequently purchased products. Further, the higher level of profitability is due more to lower costs than higher prices.

In 2002 a very thought-provoking book was published entitled *The Rule of Three*.[17] The authors concluded that if market forces were allowed to operate without excessive government intervention, there would ultimately be a consistent structure across nearly all mature markets. One group would consist of three major players ("the Big Three"), typically representing 70 percent or more of market share, competing against each other in various ways. A second group of smaller players would succeed because of their ability to carve out areas of the market where they could specialize. A third group of participants would emerge that were neither fish nor fowl, as they were not big enough to go head to head with the Big Three or sufficiently effective to compete with the specialists. The latter group would find themselves between a rock and a hard place, often competing on price, which would lead to low return on capital, as well as compromised service and quality.

If one accepts the idea that increasing market share is a desirable outcome, the next point to consider is how that increase is achieved. I prefer to see increased market share result from a superior value proposition from the customer's point of view rather than a specific corporate objective. Many of the critics of PIMS argue that seeking market share for its own sake frequently results in reducing profitability.

Most of the companies in which I've made an investment would not fall into the Big Three category. Given my preference for small- and mid-cap companies, many of them could be classified as specialty companies. Their approaches to success are typically quite different than those of the industry leaders. Jagdish Sheth and Rajendra Sisodia outline a strategic framework for specialists consisting of attributes such as keeping the specialty pure, target marketing, offering great service, minimizing fixed costs, and controlling growth. The authors underscore their belief that exclusivity is the key to market dominance of a specialty company. Achieving and maintaining market dominance for product companies requires the allocation of resources to productive R&D and proprietary technologies; on the other hand, market specialist companies need to develop a deep understanding of their best customers through an unwavering commitment to relationship marketing.

Yet another aspect of market leadership also warrants discussion. For many years I've been attracted to companies with a sharp focus on the core business. Developing and introducing new products is an exciting activity, but beware of companies that commit significant resources to new products and services that clearly fall outside the core business. Of even greater concern is a decision to acquire a company with little, if any, relationship to the core business. In 2001, Chris Zook, a consultant with Bain and Company, published a book entitled *Profit from the Core*.[18] The book focused on the importance of creating and maintaining a strong core business as a foundation for driving company growth. Analysis of the author's research leads to the following paradox: from focus comes growth; by narrowing scope, one creates expansion. Some of the conclusions reached by Zook are: (a) most companies that sustain value creation have only one or two core businesses; and (b) diversification is associated with lower average valuations than are typical of companies with focused core businesses. Of greater significance is the realization that focusing resources on the core improves the odds of achieving market leadership, which leads to increasing returns on capital. Data from 185 companies in thirty-three industries studied by Bain indicated that market leaders achieved a rate of return on capital ranging from 22.1 percent to 25.45 percent as compared to an overall average of 14.3 percent. These returns help explain why publicly owned companies whose primary focus is on the core business exhibit above-average valuations.

A Large and Loyal Customer Base

When I served as CEO of a life insurance company, I would frequently use the phrase "Nothing happens until the sale is made." And one should add, "There's no sale without a customer." A large and growing base of loyal customers is tangible evidence that a company is doing the right things as well as doing things right. The legendary Peter Drucker said, "The only profit center is the customer." Marketing has been defined as "the art and science of finding, keeping and growing profitable customers."[19] Above-average revenue growth for a specific company is much easier to achieve when new products and services are introduced to customers who have been enthusiastically waiting for new offerings and are prepared to buy.

While a large customer base is advantageous, of even greater significance is a loyal customer base. Customers who are truly loyal are repeat customers, and the longer the relationship between a company and a customer, the more profitable the customer becomes. Longer-tenured customers are more profitable for these reasons:[20]

- once customers have established a relationship with a provider they continue to buy, in part because of inertia;

- the cost of serving a retained customer declines over time;

- highly satisfied customers frequently mention the company to other potential buyers; and

- longer-term customers are less price sensitive.

Obviously, a company cannot have repeat customers without having first-time customers. However, the benefits inherent in having a loyal customer base demonstrate the degree to which companies should allocate adequate resources to achieve a high degree of customer retention.

Several years ago a leading expert on customer loyalty revealed the results of a very interesting and thought-proving study. Frederick Reichheld concluded the best indicator of revenue growth could be captured in the answer to one question: "Would you recommend this company to a friend?" Therefore, in addition to determining a company's commitment to maintaining customer loyalty, an individual investor should step back and ask, "Would I recommend the products offered by the company under consideration to a friend?" If the answer is no, that could be a red flag leading to the decision to avoid investing in the stock. On the other hand, if the question can be answered in the affirmative, one should proceed with the evaluation.

An Effective Distribution System

To be successful a company must have a product or a service that satisfies a need or a want and represents good value. However, with few exceptions it is becoming increasingly difficult and unlikely for a specific product to provide sustainable competitive advantage. When a new product or an existing product with new features is introduced, the competition follows with a similar offering within a short period of time. This phenomenon appears to exist in all industries whether manufacturing, financial services, entertainment, or health care. When a buyer or consumer demonstrates a preference for a particular product or type of service, competitors become aware and respond accordingly. Product differentiation, therefore, while important, is short lived and cannot be relied upon as a critical source of uniqueness for a company. Yet differentiation continues to be the fundamental path to competitive advantage, which prompts this question: what else is available besides the uniqueness of a product or service?

One answer to the question can be found in examining what some companies are accomplishing through the services offered that surround the product. And when the source of differentiation becomes a bundle or package of products and services, the distribution channel and how it's managed is critical. In an article published several years ago by Evan Hirsh and Steven Wheeler of what is now Booz Allen Hamilton, the authors made the following statement: "A channel can be defined as how and where a product (or service) is purchased and how and where the product is used. It is the essence of how customers and the product interact. It is the route to and the ongoing relationship with the customer."[21] Distribution channels take on a variety of characteristics, and they are a fact of life in all business sectors and all industries; but they must add value, and how the channels are managed and utilized is an important factor in determining business performance and achieving sustained competitive advantage.

In terms of evaluating the element of uniqueness in a company's distribution system, an investor should look for attributes that facilitate an intimate knowledge of customer needs, desires, and feedback with special emphasis on convenience, features, and after-sales service. Additionally one should determine if more than one channel is appropriate to reach a variety of customer segments. Making differentiation both meaningful and long lasting involves much more than the product; it must include an effective approach to how, when, and where the product or service is delivered to the customer. The more unique the approach the more likely success will follow.

Other Areas of Significant Uniqueness

In addition to the attributes that have already been discussed, there are others worthy of mention that represent the potential for significant uniqueness. Having the distinction of being the lowest-cost producer in a given industry has its challenges, but it also gives the company clout in the marketplace because of its ability to establish very competitive prices while maintaining acceptable profitability. Being the lowest-cost producer is particularly important for companies competing in a commodity-oriented market. At the other end of the spectrum is the need for devoting resources to what is intended to be a productive research and development effort. The importance of research and development varies by industry and by company, and there is evidence that R&D, as a percentage of sales for example, is not always a good indicator of the level of new offerings and their ultimate success in the marketplace. In some industries, patents are extremely important. The pharmaceutical industry has for decades benefited from strong patent positions in that prices and profit margins of ethical drugs are protected during the life of the patent. Some companies are in the unique position of having access to low-cost or high-quality natural resources, and accordingly have a competitive advantage because of that. In some instances the differences can be so significant that a quasi monopoly position exists. There's growing recognition regarding the potential importance of content. Access to one-of-a-kind databases can generate significant recurring revenues and net income. If such databases are difficult for others to produce, the longer-term benefits are extremely attractive.

Chapter Summary

- In this chapter, uniqueness is defined as one or more attributes or characteristics of a company that range from unusual to one of a kind. It is an important consideration in that uniqueness can shape differentiation and establish and maintain competitive advantage.

- Uniqueness can exist in many forms; among those most likely to be of significance in terms of sustainable competitive advantage are market or segment leadership, effective distribution, innovation, brand image, and customer loyalty

- A company whose operational activities are integrated with and supportive of the organization's strategy when combined with other significant unique attributes offers the best opportunity for above-average profit margins and investment returns.

- Focusing on the core business is vital to business success and improves the odds of achieving market leadership. Most companies that are able to sustain shareholder value creation have only one or two core businesses.

- One question that every individual should ask before investing in a company is "Would I recommend the products offered by this company to a good friend?"

CHAPTER FOUR
Leadership and Management

B enjamin Graham is the acknowledged father of investment
analysis. In his famous book, *Security Analysis*, only a few pages
are devoted to the subject of appraising management effectiveness.
However, Professor Graham did acknowledge the importance of
management, stating, "Undoubtedly the evaluation of management
will make further progress in the years to come."[22]

Profound in his thinking, though less well known, was an investor
by the name of Phil Fisher (now deceased), who remained active well into
his nineties. Mr. Fisher used a more qualitative approach to investment
analysis and acknowledged a clear and enduring bias for appraising the
effectiveness of management before making an investment. An article
about the veteran investment advisor published by *Forbes* magazine in
1996 quotes Fisher: "I have stressed management, but I haven't stressed
it enough."

It's been suggested that Warren Buffett's thinking has been shaped
by both Graham and Fisher. Buffett studied under Graham and for a
while relied heavily (with success) on evaluating balance sheets and

income statements as his preferred approach to identifying stocks selling below their intrinsic value. However, more recent evidence of Buffett's application of criteria resembles what Fisher advocated. How else can one explain his investments in Coca-Cola and Gillette, the stock prices of which consistently sold at several times book value?

My belief, reflected in this book, is that in the investment environment of today and the future, superior results will involve a disciplined approach to stock selection that relies on both qualitative and quantitative tools. And if one accepts the notion that people are primary in determining corporate outcomes, appraising the quality of management is an important and necessary qualitative device to have in one's analytical tool kit. This isn't to say that evaluating management will ever be easy or precise. It will be especially challenging for individual investors, whose time and analytical resources are more limited than what is available to professionals; but making an informed judgment about the future effectiveness of those who are managing the corporation is essential. The effective use of decision tools and criteria will pay significant dividends.

Until recently little attention has been given to differentiating between the tasks of leadership and those of management. There is a growing recognition of the difference between the two concepts and an increased appreciation of the fact that the effectiveness of both is necessary to successfully run a corporation today, regardless of size or industry. The right combination of leadership and management skills will ultimately contribute to a sustainable competitive advantage. The absence of one or the other will lead to mediocre performance, and in today's highly competitive environment, if both leadership and management skills are in short supply, one has the makings of a potential corporate and investment disaster.

The concept of management originated in the late 1800s and has developed steadily ever since, particularly since the end of World War II. In general terms the modern management process involves the core functions of (1) planning and budgeting; (2) organizing and staffing; (3) producing something of value; and (4) controlling and problem solving. These functions produce consistency and order, conditions that are necessary in the execution of day-to-day operations. Effective management is essential in producing acceptable outcomes—whether manufacturing a product or providing a service—on time and within budget. We also know that employees and managers have need for consistency and order. A corporate environment that lacks stability and predictability often produces unnecessary anxiety and contributes to a general impression that management and the corporation do not have their acts together.

On the other hand leadership is a concept that has been discussed and debated for centuries. In today's environment, effective leadership does not produce consistency; it causes movement and change.[23] Effective leadership sets direction by developing a vision of where and what the corporation should be in the future. Leadership aligns people with the desired goals and objectives of the company and produces the necessary commitment to get the job done. Effective leadership also motivates and inspires so that employees and managers are kept moving in the right direction, despite the natural barriers of bureaucracy and resistance to change. The two concepts—management and leadership—are separate yet interdependent. When combined and integrated they represent a powerful combination, and they are fundamental to outstanding corporate and investment performance.

A noted authority on the subject of leadership is Professor Warren Bennis, who has interviewed hundreds of individuals in a variety of leadership positions and written several books on the subject. In a speech to life insurance CEOs in the early 1990s he stated, "Leadership is the key determinant in the success of any institution."[24] Although that statement may not be particularly surprising, the importance of leadership in an organization has frequently been overlooked. In the hundreds of brokerage reports I've read, little was said about the qualities and characteristics of the key executives who were leading these organizations. If, as it's been stated, every organization is the shadow of a man (or a woman), why is it that so little attention is paid to the leadership qualities within the company being considered as an investment? One answer is that effective leadership is often taken for granted. We assume that a company's board of directors has selected the right person as chief executive officer and that he or she, in turn, has picked talented and effective people for other key positions. Another answer might be that assessing management is an extremely difficult and subjective task. It takes hard work, lots of time, and the benefit of a perspective not readily available to investors who are outsiders.

Leadership is so important, especially at the CEO level, because above-average corporate performance is not likely to occur with a mediocre management team in charge. New developments in the marketplace or new opportunities to serve customers do not go unnoticed or ignored for long, and companies that are effectively led respond quickly to solve problems or seize opportunities. One of my favorite lines about the role of leadership was written by John Gardner, who states that the two tasks at the heart of the popular notion of leadership are goal setting and motivating. He quotes a high school senior who said, "Leaders point us in the right direction and tell us to get moving."[25]

With leadership being so important, it's essential to become more familiar with successful leadership models. If the quality of the leadership in a company is an indicator of how attractive the returns will be to investors, it's important that we identify some specific, recognizable characteristics of an effective leader. Leadership has been discussed for centuries, and one point on which most people would agree is that leaders come in all shapes and sizes and from all walks of life. Some are born and others are made, but, according to Bennis, all seem to share some, if not all, of the following ingredients:[26]

- Vision: The leader has a clear idea of what needs to be done and the strength of purpose to do it in the face of setbacks or failures.

- Passion: The leader loves what he does and enjoys doing it. The leader who can effectively communicate this passion gives hope and inspiration to his managers and employees.

- Integrity: This characteristic—represented by self-knowledge, candor and maturity—is the basis of trust, and is the one quality that must be earned from coworkers and followers.

- Curiosity: The leader is interested in everything that impacts his world. He wants to learn as much as he can and constantly probes for meaning in what is encountered.

- Daring: A leader is willing to take risks, experiment, and try new things. She accepts and is comfortable with the notion that important insights are gained even from good attempts that turn out to be unsuccessful from a commercial point of view. Adversity is viewed as an opportunity to learn and increase proficiency.

Information about the leadership of the company being considered for investment should be analyzed with these characteristics in mind. The more persuasive the evidence of strong leadership, the more compelling the reason to look favorably on the company's stock as a vehicle for above-average investment gain. There have been and will continue to be investment opportunities that look very appealing from a quantitative point of view, but if the management of a corporation is incapable of leading effectively, there is little reason to expect that corporate performance will be sustained and that stockholders will experience significant gains.

The Ideal Leadership Team

In today's business environment of executive turnover, recruitment of CEOs from outside companies, and reports of resignations, firings, and management shake-ups, it is difficult to imagine what a near-perfect model of a corporate management team might look like. Nonetheless, creating such a model is a place to begin. In confronting this issue I consulted the research conducted by Jim Collins for his book *Built to Last* and discovered the pervasiveness of the idea of "homegrown" executives (or, stated another way, those promoted from within).[27] The research findings were startling in that only two of the "visionary" (Collins's definition of *great*) companies between 1806 and 1992 hired a CEO directly from outside the company. Collins concluded that it was not just the quality of leadership that separated the visionary companies from the pack; rather the *continuity* of quality leadership made the difference. This finding resulted in my thinking that the ideal team would consist primarily of talented executives who have been in and around an organization for many years.

Key positions in the ideal team should be occupied by individuals with strong professional and academic credentials. For example, the chief financial officer, the senior marketing officer, the chief information officer, and the human relations executive should bring an array of talent, skills, and experience that complement and raise the overall competency of the team.

Another characteristic of the ideal team is an environment that fosters active debate and discussion among team members without fear of reprisal or embarrassment and a clear expectation of respect for each individual as a behavioral norm. Although every member of an executive team has a responsibility to support and preserve such an environment, the CEO has a major responsibility for leading by example and establishing expectations for the group.

A fourth characteristic of a high-functioning team is the track record of the company. While historical results are a lagging indicator, the performance record of the company relative to its peer group and competitors is a legitimate and useful indicator of the quality and effectiveness of senior management.

An individual investor will not be able to develop an informed opinion about all of these characteristics. However, documents in the public domain, such as the annual report, Form 10-K, and annual proxy statements will reveal important information about senior executives' years of service and professional backgrounds. The track record of a company and how it compares to other companies can be readily obtained.

Indicators of Effective Leadership

It is one thing to find a corporate CEO and the leadership team with the ingredients Bennis cites; it is quite another to find visible and credible evidence of management having put into place the philosophies, strategies, and systems that will drive superior results. Measures such as profit margins and return on investment, while significant, are lagging indicators. High investment returns are the by-product of doing the right things as well as doing things right. They are the result of having the right product or service with the right cost structure in the right place at the right time, available at a price that a buyer perceives as affordable and a good value.

Indicators such as return on investment or return on equity are readily available and can inform investors about how well management has performed. However, there are countless examples of how record earnings have been followed by precipitous declines in stock prices.

Investors are usually looking ahead, and signs of deteriorating results, although not yet evident in the numbers, are a precursor to loss of investor confidence and a declining stock price; therefore, it is critical to identify leading indicators of corporate performance. Being able to point to and have confidence in signs that management has a sound game plan in place that will result in sustainable growth and acceptable returns is a key element in timely and effective investment decision making. Knowledge, understanding, and sound judgment are vital parts of successfully executing a contrarian's investment philosophy.

In looking for leading indicators, I've become attracted to those ingredients within a company that are related to long-term success. Of particular interest are those elements of positioning that represent the thinking and ingenuity of management. While it is essential to effectively manage the day-to-day operations of an enterprise, the ultimate test of effective leadership is having in place (and utilizing) the requisites of competitive success for the future. What follows is a description of five attributes that relate to superior corporate performance. These positioning elements should be thought of as a way of benchmarking corporate leadership. They will be discussed again in chapter 8, "The Expectation Factor," where their usefulness in determining the intrinsic value of a stock is explained. Under the assumption that performance is to a large extent the result of the collective efforts of the management and employees of a corporation, it seems appropriate to use a common set of attributes capable of evaluating management potential and serving as a valuation tool as well.

Competitive advantage

In today's highly competitive environment, product pricing is and will remain an issue. However price alone, even if it's the lowest, will not result in the sale if the buyer is not satisfied with anticipated performance, reliability, service, and support. As much as consumers love a sale and corporate buyers are motivated by discount pricing, a strategy based only on lowest price is inconsistent with superior financial performance over the long term. Since price is one of the most-discussed aspects of commercial transactions, high visibility belies its importance in positioning, unless that is the only dimension in which an organization can effectively compete. Competing effectively is a multidimensional undertaking. Meaningful, sustainable advantage in the marketplace is becoming increasingly important in generating the financial returns needed for meaningful investment gains. Therefore, one cannot assign high ratings to the quality of management in the absence of visible competitive strengths.

As a first step in evaluating competitive advantage, I propose that investors identify and examine a company's core competencies; at least a handful of them should exist, and determining that they are indeed core and relevant is equally important. Core competencies that meet a rigorous test are one dimension of competitive advantage and one measure of the quality of management.

According to Hamel and Prahalad, core competencies are a bundle of integrated skills, know-how, and technologies that meet three tests:[28]

1. They must make a meaningful contribution to customer value, representing skills that enable a firm to deliver a fundamental customer benefit.

2. They must represent a competitive difference by being uniquely superior in the marketplace.

3. They must be extendable—that is, applicable in new product areas.

The authors indicate that competition between firms is as much a battle for competence mastery as it is for market power. Core competencies are not assets in the accounting sense of the word; they don't show up on the balance sheet. Core competencies should not be confused with factories, distribution channels, brands, or patents, even though they may represent sources of competitive advantage. Core competencies are meant to identify and focus attention on the skills, technologies, and know-how that lie at the center of long-term success.

If a sufficient number of core competencies can be identified, and if there are not huge gaps between competencies that exist and are needed in the future, investors can assign management high marks for satisfying one important dimension of competitive strength. If, on the other hand, the identified competencies are not core competencies, this should count as a mark against management and a signal to investors that time might be better spent looking at other investment ideas or selling the position if one is owned.

Open-ended opportunities

One of the many tasks of leadership is developing a vision and then charting a future course capable of generating shareholder value. Ideally that vision will be based on open-ended opportunities. It has been said that when good management meets a bad business, the bad business will prevail. However, management's responsibility is to avoid the bad and select the good. A talented and effective leadership team improves the odds that a company will serve markets capable of growing over a period of many years, and ideally the opportunities being pursued will be within the core business or closely adjacent businesses. Shrinking markets present a set of different challenges where significant long-term growth cannot occur without increasing market share.

Corporate health

This attribute, though broadly defined, is based on the metaphor of human health, which improves when properly cared for and deteriorates when neglected. Investors should be concerned about long-term performance; corporate health is a way to measure the strength of performance endurance, thereby serving as an indicator of the future success of the business and the potential to increase shareholder value.

The authors of a recent article in the *McKinsey Quarterly* identified a number of characteristics that define corporate health:

- Resilience: the ability to quickly identify, devote resources to, and manage surprising and potentially high-impact and disruptive developments such as financial-market meltdowns, natural disasters, power failures, and the sudden death or resignation of key executives

- Execution: making good and timely decisions, performing the essential tasks well, and employing well-trained individuals who have a good understanding of their responsibilities

- Alignment: evidence of a common purpose that promotes a bond between management and employees, supported and reinforced by a shared vision, corporate values, and formal mechanisms such as performance contacts and incentives

- Renewal: evidence of an investment in well-chosen markets, utilizing existing know-how and competencies with the help of a formula for success that has been perfected by experience; also requires an organization capable of generating new ideas and adapting to change, both culturally and strategically[29]

These attributes make clear that corporate health is indeed multidimensional. How then can the individual investor hope to make a reasonably accurate assessment of a company's health? I have chosen as a proxy for corporate health two functions I believe to be the most consistent and reliable indicators, regardless of industry or company: marketing and innovation. One of the more succinct yet profound statements regarding the essential nature of these functions comes from Peter Drucker, who wrote decades ago, "The business enterprise has two and only two basic functions: marketing and innovation." Therefore, it's not too much of a stretch to argue that if a corporation's marketing acumen and its success with innovation are admirable, the underlying health of the enterprise is excellent.

Financial vitality

The leadership of an organization has at its disposal a range of options involving use of debt, cost structure, pricing philosophy, dividend policy, and expense management. In the end, however, two useful and easy-to-calculate metrics in the financial area are debt as a percentage of total capital and return on equity. A third metric is free cash flow, that is, cash that's generated during each operating period after provisions for capital expenditures and increased working capital. Although these measures are lagging indicators of performance, each should be regarded as a meaningful indicator of management's performance, as each one is a residual of successfully executing the business plan. Low debt ratios, high ROE, and generous free cash flow should be regarded as highly credible measures of management's past performance.

Earnings continuity

Investors in publicly owned companies are attracted to stocks capable of generating a steadily growing stream of earnings; of equal importance is ownership of stocks with reported earnings that are not the result of inappropriate adjustments.

The Importance of the CEO

Over the course of many years I've developed a growing awareness of the CEO's critical role and the importance of his or her leadership skills. As stated earlier, the leader of any organization casts a long shadow; the choices made and the objectives achieved or missed will reflect the judgment and priorities of the CEO. However, there have been and continue to be wide differences of opinion regarding how much of a corporation's success can be attributed directly to the CEO. I would argue that CEOs can make a huge difference—either positive or negative. The management literature offers evidence that those who believe CEOs really matter are in the majority. However, a recent article in Fortune magazine quotes Jeffrey Pfeffer, a Stanford Business School professor, as saying, "Good leaders can make a small positive difference; bad leaders can make a huge difference—because they drive people out." This observation is thought provoking in that it challenges the importance of proven CEO superstars while underscoring the degree to which an ineffective leader can cause a company to underperform or in some cases fail.

If one accepts Pfeffer's assertion as valid, then the performance gap between a good and a poor CEO should be an issue of great concern. Consistent with the tenet that investment success requires avoiding the big loss, one is led to the conclusion that investors should avoid companies led by weak CEOs. Indeed, what appears to be an undervalued stock may represent a so-called value trap in that the corporation is being led by a CEO whose continued presence in that capacity virtually assures that the stock will remain undervalued. Further, a weak CEO is apt to choose weak or mediocre managers, and a weak management team is likely to produce poor or, at best, mediocre results. A passive investor, by definition, places his or her trust in the CEO of the company being considered for investment. This truism speaks volumes about the importance of choosing companies led by effective CEOs.

Much has been written about the ingredients of executive effectiveness. Late in 2006 I came across the book, *Executive Intelligence: What All Great Leaders Have*, written by Justin Menkes; it describes the core concepts of "executive intelligence."[30] The author states that executive intelligence involves the subjects of executive work, which include essential tasks; working with and through people; and assessing and adapting oneself. In addition he identifies specific cognitive skills that determine a person's aptitude and ability to achieve a high level of performance within each of the three categories of executive work. Menkes postulates that great leaders are highly capable in all three areas, and throughout recent history were not just people of action but were also capable of critical thinking, a superior thought process that leads to a realistic assessment of environments and identification of appropriate responses to central business issues. Probing, proving, challenging, asking the tough questions, and anticipating problems are the specific cognitive skills that make up critical thinking. Although difficult for an individual investor to ascertain, the cognitive skill sets associated with great leadership represent a legitimate benchmark for identifying potentially great CEOs.

I had the privilege of serving as the CEO of two different companies over a period of twenty years. Regarding executive effectiveness, I learned early in my career the importance of being a good listener. Subordinates—indeed all employees—want to be led by someone for whom they have respect; but they also want to be heard. Employees will be more accepting of a decision knowing their point of view has been considered, even if it is rejected. Being a good listener not only satisfies their need to be heard, it also provides the benefit of gathering input on a variety of subjects that may prove useful as context for a decision—big or small.

Information Sources and Techniques of Analysis

Nothing can be quite so elusive as an accurate assessment of the leadership or management ability of a person whom you may never meet in person. This is frequently the situation faced by an individual investor who does not have the time, resources, or opportunity to personally visit a company or its management team. Still, lack of personal contact does not make it impossible to learn some important facts about the leadership characteristics of a particular group of corporate executives.

The following sources of information are usually available to any individual investor:

- Annual and quarterly reports and proxy statements: These reports usually contain a message from the CEO. The content and delivery of the message speak to the priorities and philosophies of the person who sets the tone for the entire organization. Even though the president's message may reflect some fine-tuning by corporate staff and/or public relations consultants, most CEOs have so much pride in what they have written that approval of the release will not be granted until they've had a chance to read the message for both style and content. Therefore, the comments from the president to shareholders can be interpreted as being representative of the real situation. I look for a balanced report that discusses both the good and the disappointing.

- Speeches by the CEO: From time-to-time CEOs and other senior executives are invited to speak to various groups about their company or industry. Frequently these speeches are made available to anyone who requests a copy, and the contents sometimes provide insights regarding the leadership philosophy of the CEO and/or his team.

- Informal conversation with company employees and others: When an investor is presented with the opportunity to visit with a company employee or someone who knows an employee, the resulting conversations can sometimes lead to insights about a member of management—maybe even a senior executive.

- Information on the Internet: Using Google or some other search engine as a way of uncovering information regarding a CEO or senior manager is a given. You won't know what will turn up until you start looking. Simply enter the name of the executive or CEO you want to check out, and Google will display something for perusal in a matter of seconds. It's fascinating! You may be surprised at what you find.

- Quarterly conference calls over the Internet: It's now the norm for public companies of any size to use the web as a way of communicating with shareholders and investors. Conference calls available through the company website are usually held every quarter; the CEO is present for these calls, along with the chief financial officer and at times other members of senior management. The prepared remarks typically parallel news releases in terms of content. What I find particularly interesting are the Q&A sessions; during that segment of the call you have an opportunity to hear how members of management respond to questions for which they've not had the opportunity to prepare.

- Competitors, customers, suppliers, and distributors: It's not always possible to identify individuals willing to talk about the senior management of a company with whom they might have a relationship. However, in some instances a major customer or supplier who's had an extended relationship with a company being considered for investment has unusually keen insights about the people with whom he or she works.

- Articles in the press: As an example of what can be learned from an article in a newspaper, I mention the recent announcement of the selection of the new CEO of Liz Claiborne, William McComb, whose prior executive experience had been with Johnson & Johnson. The executive recruiter for the search was quoted as saying, "Bill has an amazing ability to protect the genius in an organization and elevate the ordinary." Those few words speak volumes about the new CEO's leadership ability, and this insight was available to any individual investor with access to the *Wall Street Journal*.

- Discussion with brokerage firm representative: One good reason to have a close and ongoing connection with a full-service broker is that he or she is in constant touch with the marketplace and in a position to hear the latest rumors and opinions about the management of a company. Although one must be careful about giving too much credence to hearsay, what one hears and observes once removed should never be discarded out of hand as useless information. Sometimes a comment about the CEO or a member of senior management will help connect the dots regarding the quality of the management team.

Chapter Summary

- The performance of an organization is a reflection of the collective efforts of all employees. Over time superior results are more likely if a corporation is managed by superior leaders.

- Look for a management team with considerable experience and long tenure with the organization. There is a positive correlation between continuity of management and superior performance.

- The CEO sets the tone for the organization and is in a position to make a significant impact, for better or worse. Avoid companies with weak CEOs; look for companies led by CEOs with proven critical thinking skills.

- Important indicators of an effectively managed corporation include competitive advantage, open-ended opportunities, corporate health, financial vitality, and earnings continuity.

- While there are now more resources than ever to help individual investors evaluate management, there are still limitations; therefore, common sense and educated guesses remain a part of the process.

CHAPTER FIVE
Open-Ended Opportunities

It's a truism about stock markets that investors are always looking ahead. Stock prices are established by many forces, but expectations regarding future developments and financial performance have a major influence. The anticipated growth rate of revenues and earnings for a company is one of the forces determining the price level of its shares, and expected growth rates are influenced by the dynamics of the markets being served. It's my contention, therefore, that the size of the markets relative to the size of the companies influences investor expectations regarding growth rates. I'm not advocating that individual investors avoid companies serving mature markets—quite the contrary. However, the dimensions of the market should be considered in the valuation process. I'm especially attracted to out-of-favor companies faced with open-ended opportunities.

Open-ended implies a lack of limits, but realistically, that implication is too narrow. My use of the term is intended to convey a meaningful potential to expand revenues and is based on the following assumptions:

- The market opportunities being addressed will continue to grow for several years.

- There is an opportunity for a company to increase its market share.

- Revenue growth will be profitable.

- Acquisitions are possible and, if made, should compliment the core business.

- The scale of the opportunity is large relative to the size of the company.

- The company in pursuit of open-ended opportunities possesses or has access to the required resources.

Philip Kotler, marketing professor at the Kellogg School of Management at Northwestern University, has identified a marketing opportunity as an area of buyer need and interest where there is a high probability that a company can perform profitably in satisfying that need. He has identified three main sources of market opportunities:[31]

1. Offering something that is in short supply

2. Offering a new product or service

3. Offering an existing product or service in a new and superior way

Offering something that is in short supply

This type of opportunity requires the least talent and imagination to satisfy demand, as buyers are standing in line to purchase, prepared to pay up for the product. Shortages can and do occur suddenly for a variety of reasons. However, most shortages tend to exist for a relatively short period of time, and in an open market there's an inflow of capital because of the potential for attractive returns. When market forces have addressed the imbalance between supply and demand, the situation eventually returns to normal, which once again places a premium on the application of sound business practices.

Offering a new product or service

Consumers and businesses cannot always envision the need for a new product or service. Yet, when a new product is introduced and potential users understand how it satisfies a need or want, demand is created, and a new product offering is born. Some new products are not even planned—they just happen. One example of this type of an opportunity is the now popular Post-it note, introduced by the 3M Corporation in 1980. This product was the result of an R&D project intended to find a super adhesive. The project resulted in the accidental development of a superweak adhesive, making it possible for a piece of paper coated with the adhesive to stick to a surface and then be removed without causing damage. The introduction of the first Post-it note occurred about ten years after the development of the adhesive, and today 3M generates billions of dollars in revenues from the product and its spin-offs. Who would have thought that a piece of yellow paper and a weak adhesive could represent such an open-ended (and highly profitable) opportunity?

Offering an existing product or service in a new and superior way

One of the most interesting yet challenging approaches to the arena of new product opportunities is imagining what changes might make an existing product even better in the user's eyes. One of the benefits of this approach is that demand for the product already exists, and if the value proposition improves, market share is up for grabs. An open-ended opportunity of this type can be explained and made meaningful through examples. I've chosen the motion picture business as an example of an industry that is mature but has provided and continues to provide significant opportunities for growth in certain segments. The movie industry is now more than one hundred years old. *The Passion Play of Oberammergau* (1898) was the first commercial motion picture ever produced, and other pictures soon followed. The first theatre in the world exclusively devoted to showing motion pictures was the Nickelodeon, which was opened in June of 1905 in Pittsburgh, Pennsylvania. That theatre was a great success, and thousands of nickelodeons began appearing in cities across the United States. We can conclude, therefore, that the movie theatre represented an open-ended opportunity for individual as well as corporate investors. Over the years the business has grown, and there are now in excess of 35,000 theatres. However, the movie theatre business has itself become a mature segment even though theatre formats continue to change in order to attract business.

The development of the video cassette recorder (VCR) offered the convenience of watching movies at home instead of at a theatre. Not long after recorded movies were offered for sale, video rental stores began to appear. Home Theatre Systems opened the first video rental store, in Los Angeles, California, in the late 1970s. The movie rental industry initially expanded through small, family-owned operations. However, in the early 1980s David Cook saw an emerging open-ended opportunity in rentals, and his company, Blockbuster, Inc., opened its first movie rental store in Dallas, Texas, in 1985. The store was an immediate hit, and several others were opened. Needing cash for further expansion, Cook eventually sold one-third of the company to a group of former Waste Management executives, including Wayne Huizenga, who also envisioned great opportunities for growth and expansion. Huizenga provided the leadership and resources that resulted in the successful execution of an ambitious program. After two years of Huizenga's involvement, Blockbuster had become the largest video rental company in the United States; the number of stores had increased to more than 700, sales had tripled, profits had quadrupled, and the share price had increased sevenfold. Clearly, the recognition of an open-ended opportunity had resulted in significant payoff. While the Blockbuster story has many more chapters, some very challenging, the growth of the video rental business exceeded the expectations of almost everyone.

As we've learned over the years, nothing goes on forever, and a new concept involving video rentals eventually surfaced. With the Blockbuster business model came trips to the video store, along with rental return deadlines and late fees. DVD recording technology and the development of the Internet provided another open-ended opportunity for a company called Netflix, which concluded that there was a market for renting movies online to be delivered through the US postal system.

The Netflix model eliminated return deadlines and late fees in exchange for a monthly fee paid by the customer. Netflix opened for business in California in April of 1998. Despite doubts about the viability of an e-commerce business model, the need for several rounds of financing, the delays in reaching profitability, and emerging competition, the Netflix subscriber base continued to grow from 250,000 in 2000 to in excess of six million by the end of 2006. Independent observers of the online video rental business have stated that the present customer base of more than 8 million for the industry will grow to more than 20 million in the next four to six years. Thus, it's possible that even today this business segment remains an open-ended opportunity for investors in Netflix.

Yet another open-ended opportunity for the movie industry is emerging. There is considerable buzz regarding the long-term potential of video on demand (VOD), which enables people to watch movies over cable or the Internet, or from a recorder that has received downloaded material via wireless datacasting, cable, or the Internet. Although the customer base for this form of service is still small, the potential could be large because the service is instantly available and involves no late fees, trips to the video store, or mailing-time delays. All three of the major video rental companies (Blockbuster, Movie Gallery, and Netflix) have either expressed interest in developing this distribution alternative or are actively pursuing it.

I have described the evolution of a major entertainment industry over a period of more than one hundred years during which several open-ended opportunities have emerged and produced significant gains for investors. Other industries demonstrate similar patterns as well and provide concrete evidence of the validity of Kotler's assertion that an opportunity—perhaps very significant—can emerge when an existing product or service is made available in a new and superior way. This phenomenon is a two-edged sword, however, in that the new and superior product or service may be compelling enough to take market share away from what had been the traditional approach to serving the market.

Other Forms of Open-Ended Opportunities

Discussion about and identification of open-ended opportunities typically bring to mind revenue-producing ideas related to new products, new services, or both. However, there are other forms of opportunities capable of making a huge impact because of cost savings or improved productivity, or by extending the duration of an above-average rate of growth in revenues and profits. For example the more enlightened approach to research and development adopted by Procter and Gamble, as described in chapter 3, is an example of pursuing a higher level of innovation at a lower cost, which translates to creating additional open-ended opportunities more efficiently.

Securing a patent for a technology with a strong position and broad application potential is another example of an open-ended opportunity. While not all industries have the same regard for the importance of patent protection, we know drug companies can enjoy attractive margins, high earnings, and significant cash flow for many years on drugs with strong patent positions. Intellectual property can also generate licensing fees that can finance the development of other initiatives, thereby perpetuating an above-average rate of growth and profitability.

In recent years many publicly owned corporations have improved their fortunes and outlooks by adopting business philosophies of continuous improvement. Given the scale and scope of the operations of large corporations, a company-wide continuous improvement such as GE's Six Sigma represents an open-ended opportunity because the impact is company-wide and ongoing, rather than being a localized, one-time event.

Another open-ended opportunity involves improved employee selection and development programs. These do not directly result in an increase in revenues in the short run; however, long-term business success is a function of the level and breadth of talent in an organization, and efforts to improve employee effectiveness will have a positive and long-term impact.

Finally, an effective approach to innovation and capitalizing on its benefits can have an enormous and positive impact on corporate success. Innovation can apply to systems, procedures, strategies, business models, and a host of other issues not directly related to revenue production.

Additional Perspectives

Perhaps the most important aspect of open-ended opportunities for a company is the positive impact they have on the expectations of all constituency groups: management, employees, customers, suppliers, creditors, and investors. Attracting and retaining a talented management team and employee group is becoming increasingly important, and an organization is more likely to do this when there is a valid reason for believing that the company has a bright future. Customers are more likely to do business with a company they know will be around. Suppliers are always anxious to work with a winner and are more likely to provide support when they believe the company is going to grow since that will ultimately contribute to their own growth. Over time investors are more likely to assign a valuation premium to the stock of a company that successfully implements ambitious growth objectives. Doubts regarding a company's ability to grow its revenues, or concerns about its future viability, will have a depressing effect on the stock price since investors dislike uncertainty. Recognizing open-ended opportunities that exist for a company and that are not yet discounted in the price of its stock represents the potential for significant investment returns. The potential returns are realized when (and if) the opportunities become a reality and investor perceptions change.

There is, of course, the flip side of opportunities that appear to be open ended. A market can continue to grow, but paradigm shifts, new business models, substitute or cheaper products can and often do threaten the ability of an established competitor to grow, and these factors make it possible for companies with smaller market positions (or even new entrants) to gain market share. Therefore, opportunities must be viewed as two-edged swords; they are attractive to other viable competitors. For example, computers have been viewed as an open-ended market opportunity for decades. The management of IBM was one of the first to see the opportunity and capitalize on it by developing mainframes, which became a huge and profitable business for the company, and for a period of years IBM shareholders were handsomely rewarded. Sometime later, the founders of Digital Equipment Corporation recognized an opportunity for mini computers, and for many years the management of that company capitalized on a market opportunity, as did a number of other competitors. Again, over a period of years shareholders of Digital were significantly rewarded. Then in the 1970s micro or personal computers were developed and introduced, eventually creating another large segment of the computer industry that served both the individual and the corporate market.

The advent of the personal computer marked a paradigm shift that ultimately impacted the demand for both mainframe and minicomputers and catalyzed transformational change for both IBM and Digital Equipment. As a result of this impact and change, shareholders of both IBM and Digital suffered through a period of declining shareholder value notwithstanding the open-ended opportunity of the computer industry. The point being made is that, while open-ended opportunities are important, they must be addressed in a manner resulting in product and service offerings that are truly responsive to customer needs and that represent excellent value. Moreover, especially in today's environment, there must be an ongoing effort to continuously improve a product or a service if a company expects to retain or gain market share. One's expectation should be that the management of a good company will not only recognize opportunities but will also pursue them in an effective manner.

Chapter Summary

- The potential for open-ended opportunities exists whenever demand exceeds supply, new products are introduced to serve an existing or new need, or an existing product or service can be offered in a new and superior way.

- Serving a large and existing market, even when mature, often represents the best opportunity because the demand already exists and customers are motivated to buy if there is a new and compelling value proposition.

- The most important aspect of open-ended opportunities is the positive impact on virtually all constituency groups.

- Open-ended opportunities, if recognized before being discounted in the price of a stock, provide a basis for anticipating above-average investment returns.

- Open-ended opportunities can also represent a vulnerability to established competitors who ignore the threat of new or improved offerings by competitors or are negligent in improving their own.

CHAPTER SIX

The Strategic Framework

———————————————

Every business, regardless of form or size, needs a business plan—a track on which to run. Business terminology often includes the terms *strategy* or *strategic framework*, and the need for a strategy is not hard to rationalize. First of all, every business has limited resources. Secondly, no business can be all things to all people; choices must be made. There needs to be an intentional focus on meaningful opportunities where an organization can make a difference and provide real value to the customer. A strategy helps define how a management team will compete. Another important reason for a strategy is the role it plays in communicating direction and priorities to the organization. One can never assume that every member of every stakeholder group has the same understanding of a company's strategy. Successful outcomes demand effective utilization of resources and good execution by every member of the organization; but this will not happen unless employees, managers, executives, and directors have a common understanding of purpose, direction, and expectations. *Where are we going? How are we going to get there?* These are not idle questions; they must be answered.

As someone once stated, "If you don't know where you're going, any route will take you there."

In his book *The Strategist CEO*, Michel Roberts states it is essential for management to agree to a strategy that best positions the organization to cope with the environment it faces. Roberts uses the term *strategic profile*, which he describes as the target that guides the behavior and direction of the organization for a certain period of time. That profile becomes the all-important conceptual underpinning of the business. Employing the right strategy for the times is fundamental to success, and effective execution of the strategy will ultimately determine the degree of success.

Individual investors who manage their investments based on fundamentals are increasingly faced with the need to make judgments about the strategic framework of companies. In this age of rapid change, investors must determine if company management has a viable strategy and whether it is inadvertently drifting away from its strategy or needs to make modifications because of a changing environment. If change is required, investors must ask if management has the will, skills, and resources to successfully make the change in a timely way.

Setting aside for now the challenge of evaluating a strategy as an outsider, let's establish why an evaluation is such an important aspect of the investment decision-making process. A study conducted a number of years ago by Mercer Management Consulting revealed that 10 percent of Fortune 1000 companies lost more than one-fourth of their shareholder value in a one-month period at least once between June 1993 and May 1998. The authors noted that this was a period of time without significant market volatility. But of greater significance to investors is the conclusion reached in the study regarding the reasons for the collapse in stock prices. Nearly 60 percent of the one hundred companies whose stocks declined 25 percent or more in thirty days were victims, not from stumbling financially or operationally, but from poor strategic decisions.

There are also examples of declining shareholder value caused by weak or outdated strategies that proceeded at a more gradual pace and where the magnitude may have exceeded 50 percent. Among the classic examples, IBM Corporation, was at one time the brightest of the blue chips. Speeches, articles, and books for years cited IBM as the organization whose management practices should serve as the benchmark for others to follow. Yet between the years 1990 and 1994, shareholder value plummeted. Why? The strategic profile of IBM was rooted in the tradition of the mainframe computer, but the world was moving to distributed processing. The culture and infrastructure of the organization was based on the profitability of a line of business whose fundamentals were changing. There was a need for a significant shift in strategy; however, the leadership of the organization, whose thinking had been shaped by years of success pursuing the traditional approach to information processing, could not or would not lead the changes required in strategic thinking. It finally required the objectivity and drive of an outsider, who brought the perspective of a computer user rather than a manufacturer, to focus the attention of the organization on new challenges and opportunities. Over a period of years IBM transformed, and it continues to make and sell mainframe computers, along with a broader array of products and services, all within the context of a more enlightened, customer-focused strategy.

Today every organization, regardless of size or industry, must continuously examine its strategy in the context of changing threats and opportunities unprecedented in business history. We are witnessing a communications revolution; the digital age is here. The principle catalysts are the explosion in the use of the Internet, technological advancements in hardware, and broader bandwidth. The competitive environment of a company can change overnight, which means that strategies will need to change—rapidly, at times. Therefore, investors are faced with the challenge of not just evaluating the current strategy, but also assessing the ability of management to shift when necessary.

The Mercer study referred to earlier describes several categories of risk (hazard, financial, and operational) and concludes that strategic risk is capable of bringing a corporation to its knees, with all of the implications for a significant decline in or destruction of shareholder value. Evaluating strategic risk from an investor point of view is making a judgment about the ability of a company to deliver sustained growth in shareholder value. The evaluation process involves taking a close and common-sense look at the major elements of the strategic framework, and then answering two questions:

1. Does the corporation have a clear, focused, and viable strategy?

2. Can the business plan be effectively and efficiently executed to the satisfaction of customers and other important stakeholders?

What follows is an approach to making an evaluation of a corporation's strategy from outside the company, using information and resources available to an individual who is willing to take the time and make the effort. At this point it's important to acknowledge the challenges involved in making such an evaluation. The degree to which the management of a specific company is willing to communicate its strategic thinking varies considerably. Most annual reports and other forms of corporate literature are written to put the company in the most favorable light. Therefore, it is unlikely that one will find a section in the annual report or Form 10-K dealing with strategic deficiencies. The investor must objectively assess the statements offered and then make assumptions concerning the reasons for silence on issues that relate to the future competitive vitality of the organization.

In developing an approach for conducting this strategic audit, one should begin with the premise that every company is in a race to attract and keep customers. The potential for winning is determined by competitive advantage and its sustainability. Advantage can take many forms—some subtler than others. Examples include price, product features, service and support, response time, warranty provisions, brand awareness and loyalty, and reputation of the company to name a few. The common thread, however, is that the advantage must be viewed as legitimate and important to the entities involved in the decision to transact business. Advertising may play a role in communicating the message; however, in the final analysis, sustainable advantage is determined by whether the product or service's users believe that performance meets or exceeds expectations and/or if alternatives with a better value proposition are available in the marketplace.

Customers are not the only important constituency group to be considered; other stakeholders have a legitimate interest in the strategic direction of the company as well. A company's strategy must accommodate and appeal to the interests and needs of employees, suppliers, creditors, partners, and other stakeholders as well as investors.

With the need for and importance of a strategy having been established, we are faced with the practical question of how an individual investor should approach the task of strategic evaluation. What should one look for? Where can outsiders find credible and useful information? What are some specific examples of a clear, focused, and viable business strategy?

Essential Ingredients of a Strategic Framework

In 1980 William Glueck proposed what has proven to be a long-standing and acceptable definition of corporate strategy: "Corporate strategy is a unified, comprehensive, and integrated plan designed to assure that the basic objectives of the enterprise are met." Now, it's unlikely that an individual investor would be given a copy of a company's formal strategic plan, even if it were requested. However, a good understanding of what a strategic framework might include should prove helpful in developing a general understanding of a company's purpose, customers, products, and services. A worthwhile strategic evaluation should identify where a company is going, how it intends to get there, and the extent to which the chosen direction and business model are likely to increase shareholder value.

As a starting point I will offer some criteria for determining the viability of a strategy:

- The strategy is focused, integrated, and provides clear direction.

- It is capable of delivering an appealing value proposition to customers.

- It conveys a position of competitive advantage.

- It is sustainable over a period of years.

- It can be implemented with resources that are in place or can be acquired.

The ultimate test of viability is, of course, positive results; but since many performance indicators are lagging in nature, a strategic audit is designed to identify factors that will provide an indication of things to come. In his landmark book *Managing for Results*, written in 1964,

Peter Drucker states the following: "Economic results are earned by leadership, not by mere competence. Profits are the reward for making a unique, or at least a distinct, contribution in a meaningful area; and what is meaningful is decided by the market and customer." It cannot be stressed enough that in evaluating a strategy, one must look for evidence of superiority in the marketplace. If there are no visible signs of leadership and competitive advantage, or if a previously held position of strength is eroding, one should conclude that shareholder value is being threatened as well.

Table 6-1 outlines some key elements of a strategic framework, applicable to almost any company in any industry. These elements are intended to serve as a checklist of what to look for in a strategic audit. It's important to determine if there's a business plan that makes sense in the context of the environment facing the company. Answers to questions of implementation and resource adequacy will become more apparent with a more complete understanding of the strategic framework and its implications. An explanation of each element follows.

Table 6-1

Strategic Framework

Mission	*Vision*	*Values*	*Business Model*
What is our purpose?	Where are we going, and what will we look like in the future?	How will we behave?	How will we get it done?
The basic purpose of the organization.	A description of what the organization wishes to become and look like at some point in the future.	The enduring principles of the organization that will not be compromised in good times or bad.	The approach adopted by the organization with respect to designing, producing, marketing, distributing and supporting its products and services; and how it will compete.

Mission

A mission statement doesn't need to be fancy or long. It is a high-level expression of purpose and overall direction, and should not change very often. A mission statement is the stake in the ground that defines the broad charter of the organization. If one assumes that the basic purpose of a business is to create and keep a customer, the mission statement should convey the basis on which a company intends to justify its existence in the marketplace.

Mission statements are not always labeled as such. At times an investor needs to examine published material, such as an annual report or a 10-K, to reach his or her own conclusion regarding mission. However, there are many companies who clearly state their missions, usually somewhere near the beginning of their annual reports or on their websites. A mission statement can be very broad and expansive, such as the one for Microsoft: "At Microsoft our mission and values are to help people and businesses throughout the world realize their full potential." At the other end of the spectrum are companies with highly focused mission statements.

Vision

Vision statements have found their way into management literature and practice in recent years. In fact, the concept of organizational vision is being applied in both the for-profit and nonprofit sectors. Whereas mission defines purpose, vision is an expression of a desired future state; it provides clarity with respect to direction and desired outcomes. Vision statements are not as common as statements of mission or purpose. Sometimes management is reluctant to go out on a limb and be specific regarding its dreams and aspirations for the future. However, since equity markets are always looking ahead, every investor should be vitally interested in the future direction of a company whose stock is either owned or being considered for purchase or sale.

Vision statements can take a number of forms. Some are quite specific, making it easier to measure and track progress toward the desired goals and future state. Other statements are vague and less easily measured, but they provide direction and generate excitement.

Values

The subject of values is a more elusive but still very important element of the strategic framework. Many variables influence the success of a business and the stock price of a publicly owned company. Given the uncertainty associated with many of the variables, there is every incentive to limit exposure to risks involving unethical behavior or exploitation of customers and other stakeholders.

Hardly a day goes by when one doesn't read or hear about an inappropriate act on the part of an employee or corporate executive. These acts take on several forms including liberal accounting procedures, unethical sales practices, highly questionable approaches to competing, or devil-may-care attitudes about customers. Any intentional act that has the effect of providing short-term benefit at the expense of long-term viability or competitive advantage is suspect. On the other hand investors should look kindly toward an organization that takes a short-term hit in the interest of preserving its reputation and customer loyalty. A value system is the moral compass that guides behavior and shapes decision within the enterprise. This belief provides the rationale for concluding that every investor needs to have an understanding of the values and ideologies of the company whose shares are owned or under consideration for purchase. In the book *Built to Last*, the authors state that the main distinguishing characteristic of the most successful corporations is that they preserve the core ideologies of the company while stimulating progress and change in everything else. Core ideologies define the enduring nature of the organization and remain consistent over time; they represent the glue that holds things together as a company grows, adapts, reacts to change, and resolves problems.

A corporate value system is not always laid out in annual reports, although they now mention values more frequently. It is possible to reach some conclusions about values by reading the text of published material and observing how a company has reacted to a crisis, adversity, or an opportunity. Johnson and Johnson Corporation's 1982 Tylenol scare provides one of the most memorable examples of how a company's values come into play.[32]

A statement of values, or lack thereof, will provide an investor with either a sense of confidence or a reason for concern. Life is too short to own stock in a company managed by individuals whose values are suspect or flexible depending on circumstances. On the other hand, investments in companies with rock-solid values, whose management is unwavering in the application of these values should provide assurance that problems will be satisfactorily resolved.

Business Model

A business model is also a critical element of the strategic framework, as it defines the manner in which a company intends to pursue its mission and vision, and its related goals and objectives. Business models vary by industry and company, depending on many factors including company culture, the competitive environment, available resources, scale of the enterprise, and the product or service offering. A model defines how business will be conducted, and the form of competitive advantage should dictate the model's configuration.

Michael Porter of Harvard Business School, an international authority on the subject of competitive advantage, has made the point time and time again that above-average performance in the long run is determined by competitive advantage. Porter outlines three generic approaches for achieving above average performance in an industry: (1) cost leadership; (2) product and service differentiation; and (3) focusing on a market segment or segments. He asserts that achieving a competitive advantage requires that a choice be made as to where an organization wishes to excel—cost or differentiation. A firm cannot be all things to all customers; that is a recipe for mediocrity and subpar performance, because it typically means there is no competitive advantage at all. Yet assigning priority to either cost or differentiation requires competitive parity in the other.

Given the critical nature of competitive advantage, what should an investor look for in a business model? Porter described the following key points in an article, "What is Strategy?" published in *Harvard Business Review* several years ago:[33]

- Operational effectiveness in an enterprise is necessary but not sufficient to achieve a clear and sustainable competitive advantage.

- Competitive advantage is about being different—deliberately choosing a set of activities different from that of a competitor (or performing the same activities differently) to deliver a unique mix of value.

- Sustainable competitive advantage involves tradeoffs in the product/service offering and a supportive or complimentary fit of the many activities involved in serving customers.

Porter's message is essentially this: operating effectively and efficiently is important, but what distinguishes the winners is how a company sets itself apart in other ways from competitors. When those differences improve the value proposition in the eyes of the customer, and when the differences involve activities that fit together and reinforce each other, it becomes more challenging for others to compete. Competing against one or two product features or elements of service is far easier than competing against a company whose offering is supported by well-integrated systems of activities. Emulating an entire operating system is time consuming, costly, and difficult to execute.

From an investor point of view, the idea of selecting a company that has chosen to be different has an appeal, assuming that being different provides a meaningful competitive edge. As discussed in chapter 3, a difference that results in uniqueness has another important benefit for investors. Once recognized, companies with an enduring character of uniqueness are frequently assigned a premium in the marketplace; they have a scarcity value, especially if revenues and earnings are growing predictably at an above-average rate.

There is, however, more to a good business model than doing things differently. Designing the right model requires that critical choices be made along a number of dimensions. In his book *Value Migration*, Adrian Slywotzky makes the point that if a particular business design is to succeed, its elements must be properly aligned with the needs and priorities of customers. Equally important, according to the author, is making sure the elements are consistent with each other so that the business functions as a coherent, mutually reinforcing whole. A business built on faulty assumptions will flounder or fail. However, a business model that is designed to deliver excellent value and meet critical customer needs while at the same time generating attractive returns for the company represents a powerful combination.

It is unrealistic to expect an individual investor to evaluate every detail of a business model; a comprehensive evaluation is a task for which consultants get paid large fees, and a thorough examination requires a considerable amount of time. Therefore, an investor needs to look for a shorthand method that will provide some assurance that the business model is suitable, if not ideal.

One measure that can be looked to with a degree of confidence is the overall profit margin of the enterprise relative to the average for the industry or a group of peer companies. If after-tax margins have been reasonably stable and above average, one can assume that the business model is meeting expectations. If margins are at the high end of the range and earnings growth is also above average, one may conclude that the right model has been selected and business fundamentals are being well executed. However, buying stocks that are out of favor may involve evaluating companies when financial performance is faltering, margins are squeezed, or earnings have turned into losses. Evaluating margins becomes more difficult when problems exist. An investor must examine the historical record, assess reasons for the deterioration in margins, and make a judgment regarding the likelihood that margins will be restored to an acceptable level. It should also be emphasized that margin comparisons are most valid when they involve companies within the industry or with similar characteristics. Margins vary from one industry to another. Industries that are capital intensive tend to reflect higher margins on average than industries with low capital needs.

Another indicator of a good business model is a company's market position in the industry or market segment. Although market leadership is no guarantee of continued success, achieving or losing a leadership position says something about a company's business model and strategy. It is possible that the company became the leading factor in the industry because of some unusual combination of circumstances—even good luck—but maintaining a leadership position requires constant attention to business fundamentals and effective execution of the business plan.

A third indicator of a viable business model is the degree to which a company and its management are fulfilling their commitment to serve customer needs. Much has been written in recent years about customer orientation, listening to customers, and meeting or exceeding customer expectations. What management says about focusing on the customer is important, but what management consistently *does* is even more important. A company that can legitimately boast about service excellence, high customer loyalty, or low complaint indexes is likely a company that has its strategy in place.

The underlying theme of this book concerns the benefit of buying the common stocks of good companies at discounted prices. Evaluating the strategy of a company is an important step in determining if an out-of-favor company is also undervalued. One of the interesting ironies of buying stock when a company is out of favor is the better opportunity to acquire insights and information explaining the reasons for negative perceptions about a company and its stock. Adversity and poor performance typically lay the groundwork for an analysis regarding what caused the price of the stock to be out of favor.

Chapter Summary

- Corporate strategy is a unified, comprehensive, and integrated plan designed to assure that the basic objectives of the enterprise are met.

- A wrong or outdated strategy (strategic risk) can bring a corporation to its knees and precipitate a significant decline in shareholder value.

- A strategic framework consists of statements describing an organization's mission, vision, values, and business model. The framework is a useful tool for conducting a strategic audit.

- The business model is a critical element of the strategic framework, as it defines how a company intends to pursue its mission and vision, and related goals and objectives. A model defines how business will be conducted, and the chosen form of competitive advantage should dictate the business model's configuration.

- Three suggested indicators of a successful business model are profit margins, market position, and customer loyalty.

CHAPTER SEVEN
Financial Vitality

———————————————————

Dozens of factors influence stock prices—some more significant than others. However, one factor I regard as very important is what I call financial vitality. I chose the term quite intentionally since the word *vitality* means "capacity for survival or for the continuation of a meaningful or purposeful existence." Financial vitality is intended to convey more than the attribute of balance sheet strength; it's also an indicator of the application of sound management principles and an enlightened approach to managing a business. Throughout this book I emphasize finding and investing in good companies, and one of the attributes of a good company is financial vitality.

Financial vitality can be objectively determined because of the availability of corporate financial statements—current as well as historical. Although the tendency will be to evaluate the financial condition of a company at a point in time, it is just as important to look at trends. If a company appears to meet or exceed the tests of financial strength as of the most recent financial statement, but the long-term trend has been a weakening of these measures, this may signal problems to come. A weakening financial condition does not usually occur over night. (However, I can recall being a shareholder in a company where, because of the acquisition of a large competitor for cash and the issuance of a significant amount of debt to finance the acquisition, the financial condition and vitality of the company changed significantly in an instant—the day the acquisition closed.)

I find at least four significant measures useful in defining financial vitality: liquidity, capitalization, profitability, and free cash flow. I attach great importance to financial vitality because I believe that when a stock is out of favor there's no substitute for a strong balance sheet and good prospects for an above-average return on capital. If financial weakness is the real reason why a stock is out of favor, we need to recognize that a completely different set of challenges exists, many of which are beyond the ability of an individual investor to influence or evaluate.

Liquidity

The term *liquidity* refers to the ability to quickly turn an asset into cash without experiencing a price discount. One indicator of a company's short-term liquidity is its current ratio (the ratio of current assets to current liabilities). As a rule of thumb, a company with a strong balance sheet will have a current ratio of two to one or greater. However, this ratio will vary from company to company depending on business type and management's priorities. Another measure of liquidity is the quick ratio, which is computed using this formula:

$$\text{quick ratio} = (\text{cash} + \text{receivables} + \text{short-term investments}) / \text{current liabilities}.$$

A ratio of less than one represents a potential inability for the company to satisfy its creditors on a timely basis, which could lead to credit tightening and/or borrowing limitations. A weak liquidity position could cause a stock to fall into disfavor.

Interestingly, an out-of-favor company whose stock price has declined significantly may actually have a relatively large cash position. I have purchased stock in a company where the total of cash and equivalents was close to 50 percent of the market value of the company.

A cash position that large provides the corporation with staying power and the flexibility to deal effectively with adversity, which may include a significant stock repurchase program. An indicator of a strong liquidity position is total cash plus equivalents that exceeds the level of current liabilities.

Capital Structure

Although liquidity is an important consideration in assessing financial vitality, the strength of the balance sheet is also of great importance. A conservative capital structure (no debt or only a modest amount) provides the corporation with the flexibility to expand operations, make acquisitions, and/or repurchase stock by way of short- or long-term borrowing. A heavily leveraged company that happens to be out of favor has fewer options and thus may prove to be less attractive as a candidate for purchase.

The ratio of debt to shareholders equity is one way to describe the capital structure of a corporation. When debt exceeds the net worth of a company, I begin to lose interest in buying the stock. I prefer debt to be a very small percentage of shareholders' equity, depending on the industry and type of business. The most ideal situation is an out-of-favor company that has no debt at all. The reason for this position is my belief that a company experiencing adversity must be able to demonstrate staying power and have the necessary financial resources to see its way through a period of challenge and uncertainty.

Having a reasonable amount of debt in the capital structure is an appropriate way to finance the growth of a company, and the existence of debt should not automatically preclude consideration of a company's stock for one's portfolio. Limiting the number of names in a portfolio affords an investor the luxury of being very selective in choosing the stocks to own; so it makes sense to purchase the stock of companies with a strong balance sheet and above average liquidity.

Return on Invested Capital

We take for granted that every corporation incurs expenses. Salaries, rent, raw materials, utilities, and taxes are all essential costs related to being in business. What is sometimes overlooked, however, is the cost of capital—also a relevant cost of doing business. A widely accepted theory asserts that if the return on invested capital (ROIC) is consistently less than the cost of capital (COC), the firm is headed for extinction. Similarly, a company's value depends on its ROIC and the ability to grow. Therefore, stock selection should occur on the basis of identifying companies whose ROIC does or has the potential to exceed the COC.

For perspective on these issues, consider the results of a study conducted by McKinsey spanning a period of forty years (1963–2003).[34] Over that period of time the median ROIC of companies in the study remained quite stable at 9.0 percent even though the cross-sectional spread of ROICs widened. One-half of the companies had ROICs between 5 and 15 percent, and 84 percent of the sample had ROICs below 20 percent. ROICs varied widely by industry as well, with pharmaceuticals leading the pack at 18.4 percent and utilities being the lowest at 6.2 percent.

It is quite likely that a company whose stock is out of favor has experienced a decline in earnings and, therefore, a decline in its ROIC as well. The challenge for an individual investor is to develop a conviction that a company whose stock is a candidate for purchase can recover its earning power and sustain an ROIC that is well above its COC. In that regard, an investor's expectations about returns should be consistent with a company's core competencies, its competitive advantage, its historical performance, and the economics of the industry and market segments in which it operates. There is also evidence that individual companies' ROICs regress toward a mean over time; however, the data also shows that companies earning very high returns are more persistent in sustaining those high returns over a period of many years.

Free Cash Flow

A fourth measure used in evaluating financial vitality is free cash flow, defined as earnings after tax plus depreciation and amortization less capital expenditures and increased working capital. Free cash flow represents a discretionary resource that can be used for payment of dividends, repurchase of stock, acquisitions for cash, and expansion into new areas. Warren Buffett has defined free cash flow as owner earnings, and it forms the basis of how he determines the intrinsic value of a corporation. It is a measure less susceptible to manipulation, and to some it is more representative of financial performance.

Adding back any interest charges incurred by the corporation to free cash flow results in a measure called net cash flow from operations, which is used in the traditional discounted cash flow approach to valuation. While the discount rate is an important consideration in the valuation process, it is obvious that a corporation with the ability to generate significant amounts of cash will usually be accorded a higher value than a peer company even though reported earnings may be about the same. The level of free cash flow is a critical factor in evaluating financial vitality and determining intrinsic value.

Other Considerations

Although the measures just described are important and provide a method for objectively evaluating financial vitality, they are lagging indicators, a rearview-mirror perspective. In reality, financial policy and strategy as well as financial performance are shaped and accomplished by people. For that reason investors must make an effort to assess the competence, experience, and skills of a company's financial management team. A chief financial officer typically holds a position of major influence in a company, regardless of size. The CFO should have the ear of the CEO, be well respected in the company, and insist upon pursuing a strategy and business plan that are consistent with establishing and maintaining a high level of financial vitality. Although it is not easy for an individual investor to fully evaluate a CFO and his or her staff, an examination of the proxy statement will give an investor at least a basic understanding of the CFO's credentials, including education, professional designations, work experience, and years with the company.

Chapter Summary

- Identify and invest in companies with strong balance sheets and above-average liquidity.

- Identify and invest in companies with the potential to achieve and sustain a return on invested capital that is significantly in excess of the cost of capital and validate the reasons for the positive spread.

- Assumptions and expectations regarding future returns must pass a reality test based on competitive advantage, performance of peer companies, and industry economics.

- Although companies significantly lacking financial vitality may appear cheap, they should be avoided in a portfolio with a limited number of issues; rectifying the problem may be costly in terms of dilution of ownership, loss of competitive position, and overall momentum.

- Be satisfied that members of the company's financial management team are experienced and highly competent.

CHAPTER EIGHT

The Expectation Factor

Over a period of several years I've developed a tool designed to assist in and refine the determination of fair value for the price of a common stock. I've developed this approach with a view toward simplicity and ease of application. Although discounted cash flow may be the most theoretically correct valuation method, many other subjective factors influence the determination of fair value and the price of an individual stock. I refer to my tool as the Expectation Factor or EF.

Once the value of EF (a number ranging from 0.5 to 1.5) has been determined, it is used to adjust the output of a stock valuation model, either up or down, by direct multiplication. For example if a model were to produce a stock price of thirty dollars per share and the value of EF were 0.8, the adjusted valuation would be twenty-four dollars (0.8 × $30). The chosen outside limits for EF are arbitrary; however, the range seems to be sufficiently broad to accommodate most situations.

As initially conceived, the tool aids investors in determining if an actual stock is undervalued or overvalued. After working with the tool

I've concluded it can also be used to help make valuation comparisons with other companies being considered for investment, as well as measure the effectiveness of corporate management. EF is determined by evaluating the strengths and weakness of a company in each of five areas, referred to as attributes:

1. Competitive advantage

2. Open-ended opportunities

3. Corporate health

4. Financial vitality

5. Earnings continuity

These five attributes have been chosen through observation and experience. Other attributes also influence valuation, but these five seem especially significant. Each of the attributes were outlined and discussed in chapter 4 or alluded to in other chapters; however, a summary of them and why they are relevant follows.

Competitive Advantage

No company is without competition, and the ability to generate meaningful profit margins and achieve above-average growth in both revenues and earnings is a function of a strong competitive profile and the ability to sustain it. Competitors quickly grasp what's succeeding in the marketplace, and most are able to develop responses in a short period of time. Therefore, a competitive strength may be short-lived and needs to be enhanced. Effective barriers to entry and a commitment to continuous improvement of products and services are essential to remaining strong competitively. Chapter 6 discusses competitive advantage in more detail.

Open-Ended Opportunities

The rate at which investors are willing to capitalize earnings is determined, in part, by the size of markets being addressed and expectations about the rate and duration of growth in revenues. Declining markets may represent a short-term opportunity for a company to generate profits, but expectations about future growth opportunities create investor optimism and raise price-earnings ratios.

Corporate Health

This attribute is broad based and is a way of evaluating the ability of a corporation to sustain current performance well into the future. The health of a corporation, using this attribute, could be measured against a number of characteristics. However, since the business enterprise has only two basic functions—marketing and innovation—as proposed by Peter Drucker, they have been selected as the most important measures of corporate health and the ability of an organization to execute its plans, generate new ideas, and adapt to change.

Financial Vitality

As suggested in chapter 7, individuals who invest in out-of-favor companies should not assume the risk of significant financial weakness; there are too many other variables to be concerned about. A strong balance sheet, positive free cash flow, and returns exceeding the cost of capital represent the critical elements of financial vitality.

Earnings Continuity

One of the harsh realities of investing in publicly owned companies is the desire on the part of investors for a very steady progression of earnings per share. Highly volatile earnings usually results in a lower valuation. A smooth progression of earnings followed by a major decline usually requires several years before valuation ratios return to historical norms. Investors must, therefore, take earnings continuity into account when determining fair value.

Each attribute is evaluated using qualitative criteria presented in Exhibit 8-2 and then assigned a numerical rating of 1, 3, 6 or 9. The stronger the attribute, the higher the rating, but only one of the four numbers (and nothing in between) can be used. Once each attribute is assessed, the ratings are totaled, and then a final adjustment (not to exceed plus or minus three points) is made, and the score (S) is used to determine the Expectation Factor. The adjustment is used to compensate for what may seem to be an overly liberal or conservative assessment of one or more of the attributes. The equation is constructed to produce an EF that always falls within the range of 0.5 to 1.5.[35]

$$EF = (S^2/3000) + (S/120) + 0.45$$

Chart 8-1

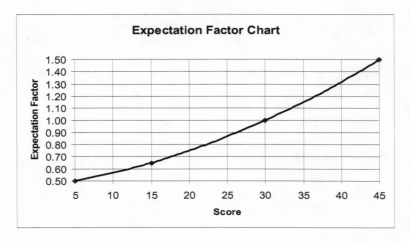

In developing an Expectation Factor, one should avoid accepting the value as being precise. It should be viewed as an expression of bias for assigning a premium or a discount to the output of a stock valuation model. In determining an EF, applying good judgment and common sense is an integral part of a process intended to provide a quantitative dimension to a qualitative evaluation.

Table 8-2

Valuation Attributes	
Competitive Advantage	**Open-Ended Opportunities**
Unique Strengths: • Scale • Customer loyalty • Intellectual property • Brand equity • Proprietary technology • Know-how • Switching costs Sustainability: • Effectiveness of competitive barriers • Speed of execution • Maintaining market leadership position	Scope: • Size of markets relative to size of corporation • Growth rates • Fit with core business Longevity: • Anticipated duration of demand curve • Time remaining before inflection point
Corporate Health	**Financial Vitality**
Culture of Innovation: • Consistent new product introductions • Enhancement of existing products • Willingness to replace or make obsolete existing products and services • Commitment to R&D Marketing Savvy: • Existence of highly qualified marketing executive • Demonstrated customer focus • Strong brand awareness • Outstanding value proposition	Return on Capital: • Returns consistently exceed cost of capital • Relationship to peer companies Capital Structure: • Debt as percent of equity • Ability to service debt under adverse conditions • Relationship to peer companies

Valuation Attributes	
Continuity of Earnings	**Comments**
Duration: • Consecutive years of increase Variability: • Range of year-to-year change • Relationship to peer companies • Relationship to market • Allowance for special charges	Using the descriptors as a guide, evaluate each attribute of the Expectation Factor. Then decide, based on the two major dimensions of each attribute, which of the four ratings should be assigned: 1, 3, 6, or 9 (nothing in between). After all five attributes have been rated, add the ratings together to arrive at an overall score. A plus or minus adjustment of up to three points can be made, and the adjusted total score will determine the Expectation Factor using the equation.

Table 8-3

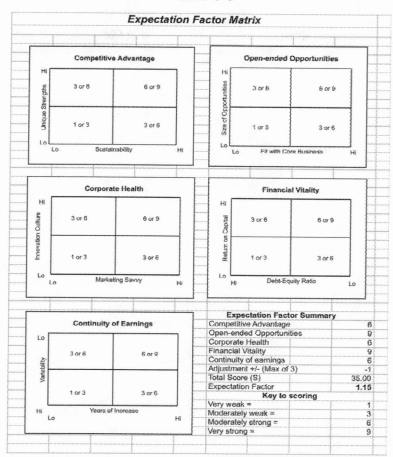

Expectation Factor Matrix

Expectation Factor Summary	
Competitive Advantage	6
Open-ended Opportunities	9
Corporate Health	6
Financial Vitality	9
Continuity of earnings	6
Adjustment +/- (Max of 3)	-1
Total Score (S)	35.00
Expectation Factor	1.15
Key to scoring	
Very weak =	1
Moderately weak =	3
Moderately strong =	6
Very strong =	9

Applying the Expectation Factor: An Example

I have chosen to use stock for a retail company (Chico's FAS, Inc., a women's apparel company) in an example of applying the Expectation Factor to the output of a valuation model. The following assessment of the five attributes for Chico's uses the evaluation matrix shown in Table 8-3, which provides the basis for arriving at a numerical rating for each attribute. The sum of the ratings and the adjustment results in the total score, which is then converted to the Expectation Factor.

Competitive Advantage

Chico's is a specialty women's apparel retail chain focused on women over thirty-five years of age. The company offers its products under three distinct brands, including one dedicated to intimate apparel. The Chico's look appeals to a body-conscious woman who takes pride in her appearance. Management understands the needs and wants of the customer base and has demonstrated an ability to respond to changes in tastes and provide value to its customer in the form of current fashion and high quality at a competitive price. In examining the matrix and making a judgment about the uniqueness of Chico's competitive strengths (above average) and their sustainability (closer to high than low), the attribute is assigned a rating of 6.

Open-Ended Opportunities

Management believes there are opportunities to significantly expand the number of stores in the United States. Additionally, the company is accelerating the development of its online retailing capability. Management has stated its intentions to consider the acquisition or organic development of other specialty retail concepts. However, in the near term it is anticipated that the focus will remain on the three existing brands, the plans for which include adding outlet stores. In examining the matrix for this attribute, the expansion opportunities represent a good fit with the core business and are meaningful relative to the size of the current business; therefore, this attribute is assigned a rating of 6.

Corporate Health

Although the assessment is very subjective, after considering the factors that define innovation culture and marketing savvy, the company appears to be average to above average in both dimensions, with marketing savvy being the stronger of the two. Historically, innovation has not been as critical to success in retailing as in manufacturing. However, there are signs that future success in any industry will require a more intentional focus on finding new and more effective ways to maintain and increase customer satisfaction, whether with unique product features or services. All things considered for Chico's, this attribute is assigned a rating of 6.

Financial Vitality

Chico's has no debt on its balance sheet, has a large cash position, and until recently had a consistently high return on capital. Working capital is more than adequate; cash generation has been consistently positive, and the company recently instituted a modest quarterly dividend and announced a stock repurchase plan. There is no doubt about the rationale for assigning a rating of 9 to this attribute.

Continuity of Earnings

Earnings declined from their peak in 2005 and showed a deficit in 2008. Several quarters of improved earnings have been reported since the year of the deficit. And while earnings improvement is expected to continue, the record over the past several years reflects lack of earnings continuity. After examining the matrix one can conclude that variability is above average and the number of years of increase is very short, resulting in a rating of 1 for this attribute.

Adjustment

After examining the ratings, it appears that the rating of 1 for continuity of earnings is too severe; therefore, an adjustment of +1 has been assigned, bringing the total score to 29.

Expectation Factor

The net score of 29 translates to an EF of 0.97; virtually no change (neither premium nor discount) should be applied to a formula-driven valuation for the stock.

The inputs to the valuation model include the long-term anticipated growth rate of earnings per share (12.5 percent annually); a high-quality corporate bond yield (7 percent); and the normalized after-tax profit margin (historical average of 10 percent).[36] These three variables determine the price-to-sales ratio (PSR). The model produces a PSR of 1.9, which when multiplied by the trailing four quarter revenues per share of $10.70 results in a valuation of $20.33 per share. The valuation is adjusted for the Expectation Factor of 0.97, producing a fair value of $19.72 per share.

$$\text{Fair Value} = (\$10.70 \times 1.9) \times 0.97 = \$19.72$$

I believe in building in a margin of safety when deciding the actual price at which I would buy the stock, and that usually involves discounting the fair value by 25 percent. In this instance the buy point would be about fifteen dollars per share (at the time of writing this chapter, the market price of Chico's shares was thirteen dollars). Although I'm not an advocate of trading on a short-term basis, I find it instructive to develop a twelve-month target price for the stock being purchased. In the example involving Chico's, I've assumed a 12 percent increase in revenues over the next twelve months and no change in margins, interest rates, or the EF; all of this translates to a target price that is 12 percent higher than the current fair value, or a price of about twenty-two dollars per share.

The information used to assess EF attributes for Chico's was obtained from two sources: the Form 10-K report and a recent company report issued by Standard & Poor's, which was available via resources accessible through the Fidelity organization.

Although estimates of profit margins and growth rates are subject to wide variations, a rational approach must be employed to decide what represents a reasonable price to pay for the stock of a company. My method involves simple arithmetic and information that is in the public domain. As usual, good judgment and common sense must also be applied. The discipline of determining fair value and assigning a discount to determine purchase price limits will result in missing what may appear to be attractive opportunities; but that is the trade-off one must accept. Remember, the objective is to buy good companies at attractive prices.

As I mentioned earlier, the Expectation Factor is also a useful approach in measuring the effectiveness of management. I emphasize this because the track record of every publicly owned company is ultimately the result of decisions made by people. Therefore, the five Expectation Factor attributes also represent a measure of the effectiveness of management in terms of financial performance, design of the business model, choice of products and services offered, and markets served. Since the five attributes are applicable to the valuation process of any publicly owned company regardless of industry, the EF enables investors to compare management efficacy as well as equity valuations.

The Expectation Factor is an attempt to provide a quantitative dimension to a qualitative assessment process. Its simplicity lies in the fact that only one of four ratings can be assigned to each attribute. The extremes of 1 or 9 can be determined more easily than the ratings of 3 or 6. However, the use of only four ratings forces the evaluation process to produce something other than a middle-of-the-road result. Additionally the use of quantitative ratings forces greater objectivity. As a general rule, I am reluctant to purchase a company with an EF of less than 30 and would avoid investing in the stock of company for which two or more of the attributes have been assigned a rating of one. Very low attribute ratings indicate significant problems and weaknesses in management, both of which are inconsistent with the definition of good companies. The EF score should be periodically evaluated for companies already owned in the portfolio. When one or more of the attributes suddenly changes, such as for a company that makes an acquisition for cash and incurs a substantial amount of debt, the financial vitality attribute could change significantly, and in the extreme the rating could drop from 9 to 1, as it once did for one of the stocks in my portfolio.

Chapter Summary

- The fair value of a common stock should be determined not only by discounted cash flow analysis or price-earnings ratios but also by qualitative considerations.

- A supplementary approach to valuation is based on the assessment of five attributes and how well they've performed over time.

- How a company has performed with respect to the attributes determines the overall score that will be used to determine the Expectation Factor.

- The EF will range from 0.5 to 1.5 and can be used to directly adjust the value derived from a variety of valuation models.

- The EF can also be used to judge the performance of corporate management.

CHAPTER NINE
Insider Ownership

H ad this chapter been written twenty years ago, it would have been
very brief and made but one point: more is better. In other words,
greater ownership of stock by insiders will result in greater benefits to
all shareholders. With the passage of time new insights have emerged
regarding stock ownership by management and directors. Although
the impact of insider ownership is difficult to measure, I much prefer
investing in a company where management and the board of directors
have a significant ownership stake in the company. There is something
positive, reassuring, and desirable about a strong alignment between
the interests of management and those of investors. What needs to
be carefully examined, however, is when this constitutes a near-ideal
situation and when, on the other hand, insider ownership represents
the potential for counter-productive behavior by management from an
investor point of view.

The underlying rationale for encouraging ownership of stock by
insiders is the concept of vested interest, that is, having a self-interest
in protecting or supporting something for the purpose of personal

gain or benefit. The most direct way of acquiring a vested interest in the financial performance of a corporation is to buy its shares on the open market with hard-earned cash. There can be no doubt that a cash purchase of shares results in a real feeling of having skin in the game, and the transaction as well as the psychological impact are identical to that experienced by an outside investor, even though the amounts may be different.

In recent years, what has clouded the benefits of stock ownership by insiders is the rising popularity and use of stock options as a component of increasingly elaborate incentive compensation programs. In many situations stock ownership by management is measured in terms of the size of unexercised option grants rather than actual shares acquired by purchase in the open market or shares owned by virtue of options that have been exercised. Although it cannot be denied that stock options create a vested interest, one can argue there's a difference. If the price of the stock falls and remains below the exercise price prior to the expiration date, the option holder loses an opportunity to acquire wealth, but there is no direct hit financially; this stands in contrast to the investor who purchases shares at a specific price and stands to either gain or lose financially depending on the financial performance of the company and the valuation assigned to the stock by the marketplace. Thus, we can conclude that stock options can result in a misalignment of interests between insiders and investors.

Stock-Option Overhang

The growing popularity and use of stock options as a significant component of the incentive compensation program has created the situation where outstanding option grants represent a significant percentage of outstanding shares. This appears to be especially true with respect to small- and mid-cap companies. As the relative size of outstanding but unexercised grants increases, so does the potential for a slower rate of growth in earnings per share with its resulting impact on the price of the stock and total investor return.

A study conducted by the firm Watson Wyatt Worldwide revealed the negative implications of an excessive use of stock options. The study illustrated the potential dilution problem of stock options and described it in terms of overhang: shares available for future options plus options previously granted divided by the current shares outstanding. The study concluded that when the overhang exceeded 10 percent, total shareholder returns declined.[37] Although the study is ten years old, it does suggest that stock options reach a point of diminishing returns with respect to benefiting shareholders. The results also corroborate the views of some prominent human resource consultants and management experts who believe there is a very weak correlation between executive compensation and corporate performance.[38]

A Positive Dimension to Insider Ownership

We have credible evidence that significant insider ownership does have a positive impact on shareholder value and return. A working paper published by the National Bureau of Economic Research in April of 2007 reveals that when a firm is acquired, shareholders on average receive 55 percent more if the bidder is a public firm rather than a private equity fund. The finding is attributed to the difference in managerial incentives between private and public firms. The study concludes that managers of firms with diffuse ownership may pay too much for acquisitions for a variety of reasons, including the desire to simply get bigger, even at the expense of shareholder value. On the other hand there is evidence of little difference being paid for an acquisition between private firms and public firms with high managerial ownership.[39]

An Upper Limit to Insider Ownership

A discussion of this topic would be incomplete without raising the issue of insider ownership that approaches or even exceeds 50 percent of the outstanding stock or where there is more than one class of shares; in these cases insiders essentially have control of the company. I can think of a number of situations where the interests of controlling shareholders are not aligned with those of regular investors. For instance, controlling shareholders may have a high level of interest in and need for income; therefore, the company is managed in a way that provides a high degree of assurance that dividends will continue at the same rate or even higher, even at the expense of funding new and attractive opportunities that may eventually result in greater profits. Insiders who have control may also manage the company in a way that assures the continuation of high cash compensation programs. Though rare, there are examples of publicly owned companies in which insiders are overly invested emotionally, have a controlling ownership stake, and are unwilling to bring in top-flight managers capable of maximizing shareholder value.

The Buffett Model of Insider Ownership

Warrant Buffett remains critical of executive compensation generally and stock-option programs in particular. In his 2005 chairman's letter Buffett describes a fictitious scenario involving the issuance of ten-year fixed-price options where, under certain assumptions including the retention of earnings to be used for stock repurchase, the CEO could earn $100 million even though total after-tax earnings had declined by 20 percent over the ten-year period. That example represents the antithesis of aligning management and shareholder interests.

Buffett has stated that he personally oversees the compensation and incentive programs of the CEOs who manage his operating companies. In simplistic terms, the Buffett approach to executive compensation can be described as follows: (1) provide incentives and an environment that causes executives to think and act like owners; and (2) pay for performance in cash. Based on information gathered for the book, *The Warren Buffett CEO*,[40] author Robert Miles describes Warren Buffett's management philosophy by citing phrases contained in the 1998 chairman's letter to shareholders of Berkshire Hathaway: "No micromanagement from headquarters. No one looking over your shoulder. Complete loyalty. Ample recognition." Each manager is given a simple mission that includes the statements: "Just run your business as if you own 100 percent of it and can't sell or merge it for at least a century."

With respect to incentives, Berkshire Hathaway simply doesn't have stock options. When a company that uses options is acquired, Buffett promptly substitutes a cash compensation plan having an economic value equivalent to that of the previous option plan—end of discussion. Even though most managers of Buffett's operating companies own Berkshire stock, their shares have not been obtained because of option grants. Further, all-cash bonuses are not based on the overall results of Berkshire but rather on the operating company for which the manager has direct responsibility. Buffett has indicated his willingness to hold out the promise of "large carrots" to his managers, but the bonus calculation is symmetrical: if incremental investment yields substandard returns, the shortfall is costly to both the manager as well as to Berkshire.[41]

In summary, not only is the Buffett model unique, it also represents a stark contrast to typical executive compensation programs in corporate America. Yet the approach seems to be working well given the overall performance of Berkshire and in light of Buffett's boast that he's never lost a manager. I would add parenthetically that one reason why it works is that most, if not all, of the operating managers are wealthy by virtue of having sold their companies to Berkshire. And their reasons for staying may be directly related to absence of micromanagement and broad freedom to act. Not having to worry about quarterly earnings expectations gives an operating manager a real advantage in terms of developing long-range plans and executing day-to-day operations.

Buying and Selling by Insiders

Monitoring insider purchase and sale transactions has been a favorite sport of many investors for decades. Even today, insider activity is closely watched and reported in a variety of ways. The reporting requirements by insiders have been modified, and information is filed with the SEC and in the public domain within a few days of each transaction. Some investors, including professionals, use insider-trading information as a screening device for identifying stocks that may be attractive investments.

Although insiders are not infallible as investors, insider transactions do represent decisions to buy and sell by individuals who are in a preferred position with regard to assessing the outlook for a company—especially in the near term. Therefore, individual investors should be aware of insider transactions as they pertain to portfolio holdings as well as stocks under consideration for purchase.

With the exception of stocks purchased by recently appointed directors, who have an obligation to acquire at least a token holding, any purchase made by an insider should be viewed as a positive sign—especially if the size of the transaction is large relative to stock already owned. Several sizeable insider purchases should be initially interpreted as very bullish, although a subsequent analysis may dampen one's enthusiasm.

On the other hand, interpreting the significance of insider sales is less clear-cut. Insider sales can occur for reasons other than a pessimistic outlook, however. At some point during the career of an executive, estate planning takes a priority, and the executive will take actions that might involve reducing his or her primary holding and build a more diversified portfolio of investments. These executives may use appreciated stocks to satisfy charitable gift commitments, or the proceeds from the sale of a stock may be earmarked for the purchase of a new home or a new automobile. On balance, however, any sale activity should be viewed as a potential negative signal to the market and evaluated. Simultaneous sales of stock—especially in large quantities—by several insiders is usually a sign that trouble is on the horizon.

Monitoring insider activity can be done quickly and should be part of the ongoing due diligence process adopted by every serious investor. However, whatever signal an insider transaction sends to the market is usually reflected in the price of the stock within hours or a day or two. Therefore, my approach to insider transactions is to adopt the attitude of an observer and base my buy, sell, or hold decisions on the evaluation of other important fundamental factors such as the outlook for revenue growth, margins, and earnings per share.

Executive Compensation

Although this chapter deals with insider stock ownership, I've chosen not to pass up this opportunity to discuss a related subject: executive compensation—and, in particular, CEO compensation. This topic in recent years has taken on a life of its own, and for good reason.

Plato, the ancient Greek philosopher, addressed executive compensation when he stated that no one in a community should earn more than five times the wages of the ordinary worker. Peter Drucker became the modern-day zealot when, in a 1984 essay, he declared CEO pay out of control and implored corporate boards to hold CEO pay to no more than twenty times the salary of the rank and file. Drucker was passionate about the subject and continuously advocated the 20:1 ratio in his speeches and writings. I have not uncovered a theoretical rationale for his ratio, but clearly he was deeply concerned that too large a pay gap between CEOs and workers could threaten the credibility of leadership and make a mockery of the contribution of other employees in a successful organization. Ratios of 5:1 or 20:1 seem ludicrous in today's compensation arena where annual CEO compensation can reach several hundred times the level of the rank and file.

While one can debate the merits of a specific ratio, it's unrealistic to reject the notion that there is a gap beyond which worker commitment, contribution, and cooperation begin to break down. The cause of today's high CEO compensation levels involves four parties: CEOs, board compensation committees, compensation consultants, and institutional investors; and the chief culprit in the implementation process is the stock-option grant. If every corporation wishes to have above-average compensation opportunities, the inevitable result is a year-after-year ratcheting up of salaries, bonuses, and stock option grants.

Relatively few would argue against the concept of "pay for performance." However, a recent study published in the *Financial Analysts Journal* reveals a very troubling relationship between executive compensation and corporate performance.[42] The study, which covered the period 1997 to 2004 and involved 455 of the S&P 500 companies, revealed that when either market-based or income-based performance measures were used, companies with the highest levels of compensation reported future performance on a basis consistent with that of other companies. During some periods, by at least one measure, the performance of companies reporting the highest amount of compensation was significantly worse than the performance of other companies. Controlling the research for company size did not change the results of the study. The authors identified several caveats, including that the conclusions do not extend to specific companies or to small and midsize companies. Caveats aside, however, the study raises serious questions regarding the beneficial impact of executive compensation packages on shareholder value.

The out-of-control situation identified by Drucker in 1984 has grown considerably larger, and it may now be of crisis proportions. Although a solution to the problem of excessive compensation has proved elusive, it is thought to involve a combination of factors including a tougher approach by compensation committees, greater transparency of compensation plans and payouts, and a more aggressive stance by institutional investors and shareholder activists. In the meantime, investors should avoid the stocks of companies in which executive compensation appears to be off the chart. The rationale for this stance is the belief that excessive executive compensation eventually results in a breakdown in the alignment of interests between management and investors and between executives and the rank and file. And in the final analysis, lack of alignment will negatively impact corporate performance.

Reconciling the Pros and Cons of Insider Ownership

The reconciliation process begins with the assumption that aligning the interests of insiders (management and directors) and outside investors is vital and that the foundation of that alignment is a strong sense of ownership on the part of insiders. Over the course of many decades, considerable research has been conducted regarding the psychology of ownership in a wide variety of fields. A recent study conducted by Linn Van Dyne and Jon L. Pierce from Michigan State University and the University of Minnesota, respectively, and published in the *Journal of Organizational Behavior* demonstrates positive links between psychological ownership for the organization and employee attitudes and work behavior. Additionally the research also reaffirms the close relationship between possessions, feelings of possession, and feelings of ownership, which, in turn, trigger a sense of responsibility for the organization.[43] In summary, the researchers hypothesize that psychological ownership for the organization is related to commitment, satisfaction, organization-based self-esteem, performance, and citizenship behavior. If the research findings are valid one can conclude that insider ownership goes far beyond investor alignment.

Having established the importance of ownership, the next issues to address are the form and degree of ownership. The most visible and direct form of ownership for insiders is stock acquired for cash in the open market or by purchase of shares available through a stock option plan. Actual ownership of shares is important in that it puts a portion of one's net worth at risk just as outside investors do when they buy shares. Ownership by way of unexercised stock options is not the same as direct ownership of shares. Unexercised option grants represent a way to establish or increase ownership. An opportunity to increase one's net worth is at risk. The issue of the appropriate degree of ownership is more elusive, but most likely varies by individual. In conducting the research for this chapter I discovered a recently adopted stock ownership policy for members of the board and executive officers of the Wachovia Corporation. While not necessarily typical of the policies of other corporations, it represents the direction being taken by some publicly owned corporations with respect to minimum ownership, as well as retention guidelines regarding stock acquired through stock-option plans. The Wachovia policy regarding stock ownership is five times base salary for the CEO, four times the base salary for all other executive officers, and five times the annual cash retainer for directors.

In summary, when considering investing in the stock of a company, one must carefully examine the degree to which the interests between insiders and outside investors are aligned as measured by the actual amount of stock owned and the degree to which stock options are represented in the compensation package. Excessively large stock-option grants are a cause for concern in that they represent a potential for misalignment and a compromised outcome for shareholders.

Chapter Summary

- Alignment of the interests of insiders with those of outside investors is a desirable goal; the balance will never be perfect, but continuous improvement should be a priority.

- Insider ownership that consists primarily of unexercised stock options does not constitute a vested interest in the performance of the company that is consistent with the expectations of outside investors.

- An overhang of stock options exceeding 10 percent of shares outstanding is a red flag and represents a condition with the potential to compromise total shareholder returns.

- The design of a stock-option program will influence executive decisions that may or may not be in keeping with maximizing total shareholder returns.

- There is at best a weak correlation between the level and form of executive compensation and corporate performance; however, that assumption is not intended to contradict the importance of aligning the respective interests of insiders and investors.

CHAPTER TEN
Opportunity for Gain

In the president's letter in the annual report of a company in which I have an investment, the following statement appears: "The key to great results is high expectations."[44] The approach to stock selection and portfolio management outlined in this book is in keeping with this statement.

It's been suggested already that if one's goal is to achieve investment returns equal to that of the market, the best approach is to purchase an equity index fund, where results will approximate the return of the S&P 500 stock index or the Wilshire 5000 index. On the other hand, if you assume that proper selection of relatively few stocks of good companies at bargain prices can result in returns exceeding that of an index fund, you should establish high expectations with respect to the potential return of any investment that is made.

Over many decades, stocks of large companies have on average provided a total return of 10 percent annually. My proposal is to look for stocks that have the potential to at least double over a period of three to four years—equal to a return of more than 20 percent annually, or twice that of a broad market average. Gains of that order represent high expectations; however, since in all likelihood some investments will not meet these expectations, raising the bar to that level is necessary to increase the odds that overall results will exceed the market by several percentage points.

In today's market environment, the scenarios most likely to produce results meeting the test of high expectations include buying stocks that are out of favor with a heavy emphasis on small and midsize companies. In his book *Hedgehogging*, Barton Biggs points out that since 1927 small-value stocks have compounded at 14.8 percent per year compared to large-value stocks at 11.5 percent per year. Over this same period of time, large as well as small growth stocks have compounded between 9.2 and 9.6 percent annually.[45] These historical results suggest that a concentrated portfolio of stocks of good companies purchased when they were out of favor can generate returns exceeding that of an index fund by three to five percentage points.

Although the odds may be with investors who select the stocks of small companies, there are times when the stocks of large (and good) companies can double in a relatively short period of time. A recent example is the Hewlett-Packard Corporation. From May of 2005 to May of 2007, the stock price increased from twenty dollars to forty-five dollars, more than doubling in two years. Another example is McDonald's, whose stock increased from twenty-six dollars to fifty-two dollars between August of 2004 and May of 2007, doubling in less than three years. Both of these stocks were clearly out of favor at the beginning of the periods mentioned; however, with strong franchises, excellent balance sheets, and unrealized earning power, patient investors willing to accept the uncertainty of the moment experienced gains far exceeding those provided by the market.

Another example of investment performance exceeding the market involves stocks selected using Joel Greenblatt's Magic Formula.[46] During the period from 1988 to 2004, a portfolio limited to thirty stocks, selected from a list of 1,000 using Magic Formula criteria, produced an annual return of 22.9 percent compared to the 12.4 percent return of the S&P 500 index—a difference of more than 10 percent.

Pursuing the goal of significant gains requires discipline, fortitude, and patience. Sometimes the stock of a company identified as a candidate for the portfolio will measure up to all of the characteristics of a good company but won't be selling at a bargain price, which is critical if returns exceeding that of the market are going to realized consistently over the long term. An approach that I've taken is to look for stocks that have declined at least 40 percent from their fifty-two-week high. (I use that metric to define out of favor.) Then, after examining how a company measures up with respect to the five attributes discussed in the chapter on the Expectation Factor, I make a judgment regarding the intrinsic value of the company, taking into consideration, actual and prospective growth and profitability, the expectation factor, peer company comparisons, interest rates, and the level of equity markets.[47] Having reached a conclusion regarding intrinsic value, the next step is to compare the current market price to the intrinsic value. If a company is undervalued as well as out of favor, the current market price must be below the intrinsic value, and the gap should be meaningful. (I would suggest something on the order of 25 percent.)

By way of illustration, assume you have identified a stock that meets the test of a good company and the intrinsic value is twenty dollars, while the actual market price is fourteen dollars. Assume the intrinsic value increases at the rate of 10 percent annually and that in three to four years the market price is equal to intrinsic value, which would then be twenty-eight dollars. In this hypothetical situation, the investor owns a stock that has doubled in three to four years and realized a compound annualized gain (before dividends, if any) of about 22 percent. Discipline is required since performing the due diligence on the company may reveal an unusually unique and appealing investment opportunity from a fundamental point of view but virtually no difference between the market price and intrinsic value. There may be a great temptation to buy the stock based on gut instinct. Patience is required because it may take three or more years before the market price reaches the company's intrinsic value. Adopting the approach of owning only a few stocks provides an investor with the luxury of being very selective and continuing to look for the stock with the right combination of good fundamentals and price.

One of the best-selling books on investing is *The Battle for Investment Survival* by Gerald M. Loeb, a strong advocate of concentrating investments in a limited number of stocks (also a major theme of this book). Mr. Loeb states that diversification is undesirable, rationalizing that concentration in only a few stocks ensures that enough time will be devoted to analysis and selection so that every important detail about them will be known and understood. He also states with great conviction that it is futile to try to get superior returns except by buying into anticipated large gains.[48]

Assessing the Gain Potential: Both Art and Science

It must be obvious by now that making a judgment about the level of a stock price at some future date and the potential investment gain over a period of years is not an exact science. However, making an educated guess about the future price level of a company's stock is better than having no opinion at all. I have found examining the annual range of price-to-sales ratios to be a useful and convenient way to compare the current price of a stock to where it might sell in the future. Revenues are more stable than earnings; therefore, total revenues divided by shares outstanding will produce a ratio that will also be more stable. Dividing the stock price by revenues per share produces what is referred to as the price-to-sales ratio (PSR). Since this ratio is influenced by both profit margins and the anticipated future growth of revenues and earnings, the application of both qualitative and quantitative factors mentioned earlier can lead to a more informed assessment of the potential price level of a stock in three to four years.

By way of example, if a stock is currently selling at 0.9 × revenues and the average PSR over the past several years has been 1.3 × revenues, assuming a continuation of historical growth (assume 10 percent for this example) and no significant change in profit margins, it would not be unreasonable to expect the price of the stock to double in three to four years. This example illustrates the added benefit of buying a stock that is selling below its intrinsic value (that is, undervalued). In this case the gain in stock price from undervalued to fairly valued is significant relative to the gain in price due to the growth in revenues and earnings. Of course, profit margins and revenue growth may not be the same in the future as in the past, and if future financial performance is less robust, the average PSR ratio in the future is most likely to be less than the historical average, resulting in an investment return that falls short of expectations. However, purchasing a stock at the lower end of its historical PSR range provides a margin of safety that will minimize any loss or even provide for some gain even though expectations are not met.

Chapter Summary

- Begin purchasing a stock only after determining that the potential exists for long-term gains significantly greater than for an index fund, preferably an expectation that the price of the stock could double in three to four years.

- Identify and evaluate stocks that have declined by at least 40 percent over the past fifty-two weeks.

- Attention should be focused on stocks selling at 25 percent or more below intrinsic value.

- Intrinsic value is determined by estimating future net cash flows discounted to present value at a rate equal to the cost of capital

CHAPTER ELEVEN

Concentration

For as long as I can remember, an important tenet of prudent investing has been adequate portfolio diversification. A common interpretation has been that diversification requires having no more than a few percent of your total invested assets in one security. Many professional money managers believe there should be at least fifty to one hundred names in a portfolio. Indeed, many institutions have prescribed diversification parameters that cannot be ignored.

On the other hand, a number of highly successful investors have advocated concentrated portfolios for individuals as an alternative to the conventional wisdom of broad diversification. For example, Peter Lynch of the Fidelity organization and past portfolio manager of the Magellan Fund is an advocate of investing in a handful of securities. Likewise, Warren Buffett believes that concentration in the right companies can be a more prudent and rewarding course of action than broad diversification. Philip Fisher, a longtime advocate of growth-stock investing, believed a portfolio should consist of between five and ten names. It's also interesting to note that Benjamin Graham in his seminal 1949 book, *The Intelligent Investor*, cautioned against excessive investing and indicated that, even for the defensive investor, the number of issues in a portfolio could be as few as ten.[49]

My own belief is that, for individual investors, concentrating one's holdings in ten names or fewer, assuming each company has different investment characteristics, represents a valid and potentially productive practice. Here are the reasons for that belief:

- Less risk reduces the potential for higher returns. To achieve investment performance that exceeds that of the market, individual investors must assume greater risk (higher volatility). A portfolio of fewer than ten securities is most likely to be more volatile than the market (or an index fund), but also offers the potential for greater rewards.

- Owning relatively few names enables the individual to become very familiar with each portfolio holding. An understanding of each company owned is not only desirable, it is *essential* if one is to have the confidence necessary to make informed and timely buy-and-sell decisions. Most individuals, even those who are retired, simply do not have the time or desire to follow and remain intimately familiar with fifty or more different securities.

- Owning relatively few names imposes an important discipline. Each company whose stock is a candidate for ownership should possess investment fundamentals equal to or superior than companies already in the portfolio and should be valued at the time of purchase at a price that is as attractive or more attractive than other companies in the portfolio. If that test cannot be met, the idea should be put on the shelf or discarded.

- A stock in a portfolio of fewer than ten names will have a meaningful impact on the total value of the portfolio if the investment fundamentals have been correctly assessed and the value of the stock increases accordingly. Impact, of course, works both ways; but if a stock is purchased when it is undervalued, the impact of price change should be positive more often than negative. A stock that increases 50 percent in price and is 10 percent or more of the portfolio will have a greater impact on the total portfolio than a stock whose representation is 2 percent or less.

Thus portfolio concentration, despite the potential trade-off of higher volatility, offers the benefits of focus, familiarity, discipline, and impact, thereby improving the odds that long-term investment performance will exceed the results of investing in an index fund.

A Perspective on the Realities of Diversification

There can be no disagreement that a portfolio of several stocks offers more diversification than a portfolio consisting of only one. However, a portfolio consisting of ten or more bank stocks may be less diversified than a portfolio of five stocks, each of which is in a different industry, assuming a low degree of correlation. Therefore, a concentrated portfolio should be constructed in a way that results in a low degree of correlation between issues in terms of business and stock price performance. According to Richard Brealey, portfolio risk is a function of the risk characteristics of each individual holding; the number of holdings; and the degree to which there is interdependence between issues.[50]

Assuming adequate industry diversification, it is surprising to note how relatively few names in a portfolio quickly brings into play the law of diminishing returns. Brealey points out that risk expressed as a percentage of a one-stock portfolio reaches 74 percent when the portfolio consists of ten stocks, with that measure stabilizing at 71.4 percent with fifty issues and remaining only slightly below 71 percent even when a portfolio consists of more than 1,000 issues.[51] Therefore, one can generalize that most of the benefits of diversification can be realized with a portfolio of ten securities. It should also be obvious that the quality of diversification is as important as the quantity, if not more so; *quality* here refers to the differing characteristics of each holding in the portfolio in terms of industry representation, cyclicality of revenues and earnings, volatility of stock price, and valuation parameters.

In need of examination at this point is the issue of portfolio optimization. Is there a way to determine the number of securities in a portfolio that will result in the ideal compromise between degree of potential impact and adequate diversification? Nearly twenty years ago an individual named Robert Sharp proposed that investors consider applying the gambling rules of bet sizing to the number of issues in an investment portfolio.[52] The basis for his suggestion was the work of mathematician Edward Thorp of the University of California at Irvine, who had published work on bet sizing applied to warrants and options. Without getting into the details, Sharp's formula for determining the optimum number of issues in a portfolio is below:

$$N = L \times (R + q)/(R \times p)$$

N is the optimum number of issues; R is the expected return; p is the probability of success; q is the probability of failure; and L is the expected average loss of each losing investment. For example, if one were to assume R to be 10 percent (or 0.1), p to be 50 percent (or .5), q to be 50 percent (or .5), and L to be 50 percent (or .5), the math works out as follows:

$$N = 0.5 \times (0.1 + 0.5)/(0.1 \times 0.5) = 6 \text{ issues}$$

These assumptions might be viewed by some as too conservative; however, they are not unrealistic in that fifty-fifty odds are being assigned to success and failure (the track record of investors could be better or worse); a 10 percent return represents the long-term performance of equity markets; and an average loss of 50 percent on a losing investment may be representative of the experience of many investors whose optimism results in waiting too long before selling a holding. Sharp's experience indicated that he should assign a value of 25 percent to L, resulting in an optimum portfolio of three issues, and he went on to propose that the individual investor should never have fewer than two stocks in his portfolio, nor should he or she have more than five.

The work of both Sharp and Brealey offers quantitative support for the proposition that individual investors should seriously consider adopting a model portfolio consisting of no more than ten issues. Realizing that investing is still an art as much as it's a science, I would suggest a range of five to ten issues. In my own case I've selected seven and made every effort to adhere to that parameter, making exceptions only when changes are being made in actual names (buying and selling).

I selected seven because it allows for some reduction in the assumed rate of return (perhaps appropriate at the time of this writing) and/or a higher average loss on losing investments. A portfolio of seven issues also represents a modest reduction in risk, using Brealey's table as a basis for that measure.

Choosing the number seven is also based on another finding. For decades psychologists, behavioral scientists, and others have suggested the human mind has limits on its ability to process information. George A. Miller, in a paper published in the *Psychological Review* in 1956, discusses experiments and tentative conclusions that lead the reader to conclude that the span of absolute judgment and the span of immediate memory impose severe limitations on the amount of information humans are able to receive, process, and remember. In a number of experiments, seven units or categories of information represented the upper limits of capacity. Information overload resulted in errors of recall, interpretation, and judgment. While one might question the validity of applying these findings to portfolio theory, I would argue that if one can accept the logic of having a portfolio of fewer than ten issues, perhaps having a target of seven issues will also make sense, given the vast amount of data and information available to today's individual investor. Clarity of understanding and good judgment are important ingredients in the investment decision-making process and we should avail ourselves of every tool and technique to ensure their preservation.

Up to this point the discussion about diversification and optimization implicitly assumes that each issue in a portfolio has the same value, even though they differ in character. We know, however, that is rarely if ever the case. Individual securities rise and decline by varying percentages every trading day, and over time it's possible for a portfolio to reflect great variation in the percentage representation of each issue, even though at the outset each issue would have the same weighting. Therefore, one must explore how the reality of continuous change in individual weightings impacts the arguments made regarding portfolio concentration.

Portfolio Rebalancing

Let's assume the creation of a portfolio with seven issues, each having a market value of $100,000, for a total portfolio value of $700,000. Within two years, the value of the portfolio increases by $200,000, all because of the performance of only one issue (which, having tripled in value, now represents one-third of the total portfolio). This situation challenges the original assumptions about risk and optimization and begs the question of portfolio balance. One alternative, of course, is to rebalance the portfolio at regular intervals, thereby restoring equal ratings and maintaining the integrity of the assumptions. This alternative, however, has implications in terms of portfolio turnover (transactions costs) and taxable gains, both short and long term. The tax issue is not a factor in nontaxable accounts such as a self-directed IRA. Another alternative is to let the profits run by holding on to the stock until such time as it appears to be selling far in excess of its intrinsic value and/or represents an extreme overvaluation.

Continuing with this example, the impact of the stock that tripled in value is exactly the same as the impact it would have on a three-stock portfolio in which each holding is of the same value. Using Sharp's assumption that an optimum portfolio should consist of three stocks, one could argue that once a holding reaches one-third of total portfolio, rebalancing should be considered. Therefore, I have somewhat arbitrarily concluded that once the value of an individual stock in the portfolio reaches one-third of the total portfolio value, rebalancing should be mandatory; and if the value of a stock reaches one-fourth the value of the portfolio, rebalancing should be seriously considered, but is optional. Once the decision is made to rebalance, the reallocation of assets should be determined on the basis of the ratio of current price to the twelve-month target for each security in the portfolio. The stock with the lowest ratio should be allocated the greatest share of portfolio value. Rebalancing should result in no more than 20 percent in an issue and no less than 10 percent. Thus, in a seven-stock portfolio a potential reallocation could consist of two stocks of 20 percent each, two stocks of 15 percent each, and three stocks of 10 percent each. My own experience has been that one holding rarely reaches 33 percent of the portfolio, while 25 percent is not uncommon, depending on the size of the initial purchase. A decision to sell an entire holding and replace it with something new should not automatically trigger a decision to rebalance, although it should be considered. Each investor may have his or her idea about rebalancing, but the important principle is to avoid high turnover and being too quick to sell a company that continues to demonstrate sound fundamentals and the ability to increase shareholder value.

Chapter Summary

- A number of very successful investors, including Buffett, Fisher, and Lynch, have consistently advocated concentrated portfolios.

- A concentrated portfolio will experience higher volatility than an index fund, and year-to-year variation in performance is likely to be greater than for an index fund.

- A concentrated portfolio makes it possible for the individual investor to better understand the fundamentals of each issue and provides him or her with the luxury of being very selective in what is owned.

- Credible evidence indicates that most of the benefits of diversification can be accomplished with a portfolio of ten names. Moreover, the risk being diversified is volatility, which should be less of a concern for long-term investors.

- Achieving above-average returns requires a greater emphasis on optimization than on diversification of the portfolio.

CHAPTER TWELVE

When to Sell

K nowing when to sell is one of the most difficult aspects of common stock investing. In a perfect world, assuming that a portfolio of stocks had been carefully selected, the answer would be never. However, the investing world is far from perfect. Circumstances and conditions change; stock prices change; and management teams change. Long-term investors rely on profitable revenue growth as the basis for attractive returns, and the historical evidence regarding sustainable growth is cause for concern. A study conducted by the Bain organization revealed that in a group of 1,854 companies, only nine percent demonstrated sustained real growth of at least eight percent annually (10 to 12 percent nominally) over a period of ten years.[53]

The challenge of achieving sustained double-digit growth in earnings and shareholder value begs the question of the merits of a "buy and never sell" strategy. There is also the economic argument that, over time, a company's return on investment will eventually be reduced to its cost of capital—due essentially to forces of the marketplace. In my opinion, these realities suggest that a portfolio of well-selected stocks with zero turnover is unlikely to exceed the return of an index fund.

From an intuitive point of view it seems more rational to sell a stock when a company is having problems, and foolish to sell when a stock is going up in reaction to excellent corporate results. However, if one accepts the notion that a contrarian approach to investing is an essential part of achieving above-average returns, one should buy when there are uncertainties and sell when the outlook is positive and the stock price is considerably above its intrinsic value. One of the principle obstacles to selling is human emotion and personal ego. Proper selection of stocks for a portfolio will involve investing the time and energy needed to gain familiarity with the fundamentals and to complete the due-diligence process. After conducting research and then purchasing a position, an investor begins to lose objectivity. A positive bias favoring ownership of the stock develops and acts as a blinder, making it unlikely that a change in mind-set will occur anytime soon.

Given the psychological issues that act as barriers to considering the sale of a holding, it's important that investors have a set of rules or guidelines that will force objectivity and influence sale decisions. The rationale for selling a holding should be clear in the mind of the investor, and the decision rules should be applied consistently. There are at least five conditions, each of which might constitute a legitimate basis for selling a holding, and they are discussed in greater detail below.

Decisions Based on Flawed Logic

No investor, regardless of experience, is infallible. Incorrect assessments can be made; incomplete information or misinterpretation of correct information can lead to poor decisions. I believe it is safe to say that every investor at some time will decide to purchase a stock, only to find that subsequent events or revelations indicate that he or she made a wrong decision. One example is Warren Buffett's purchase of 8 million shares of Pier 1 Imports in 2004. The purchase was made at an average price exceeding seventeen dollars per share. About a year later, Buffett decided to begin liquidating the holding at a loss, and he eventually sold the entire position. Subsequent events have vindicated Mr. Buffett's judgment inasmuch as Pier 1 experienced a significant decline in same-store sales and an overall decline in revenues, resulting in a major loss in fiscal year 2007. Given Mr. Buffett's attitude regarding the limited success of turnaround situations, one can appreciate his decision to sell Pier 1 Imports and admire his ability to reassess what he had initially found to be an attractive investment.

The objective reevaluation of a stock that has been purchased is extremely difficult, especially if the stock price has declined. In his book *Influence: The Psychology of Persuasion*, Dr. Robert Cialdini describes how humans act they way they do and discusses six tendencies, including commitment and consistency. He states that, after making a decision and committing to it, either verbally or in writing, individuals are reluctant to change their view even when the original incentive or motivation has been removed or is no longer valid. Cialdini discusses reasons for this tendency including his belief that consistency allows individuals to avoid the consequences of reason—that we have to change, that we have to act. This psychological bias is likely present in all investors and helps explain the reluctance of many to unwind a stock purchase that subsequent analysis indicates was unwise.

Changes in Business Model

It's been said many times that change is a constant, and although the rate of change will vary from industry to industry and company to company, new assumptions and circumstances cause the management of a company to react. This reaction may be modest, or management may overreact. In some instances the competitive environment may be undergoing a paradigm shift, yet some management teams may be either oblivious to the changes or unwilling to react, for whatever reason.

If there's a significant change underway in the competitive environment or if the management of a company whose stock you own appears to be making a significant change in its approach to the market, it's necessary to make a judgment regarding the degree of change and whether or not it's right or even needed. Changes in a company's business model may occur because of a conscious decision by management, or they may be a necessary response to regulators, competitors, consumer demand, or new circumstances.

Eastman Kodak offers an example of the need for a new business model. This company dominated the traditional photographic film and processing market for decades. Kodak was in the enviable position of serving a growing and highly profitable market with products and services that involved recurring revenues. And then along came digital photography—a technology that changed everything. Traditional photography involved the production and sale of consumables—film, paper, and chemicals. Digital photography involved hardware, software, and services (and most recently for Kodak, consumable inks for printers). A successful transition from the old to the new requires a different business model, and the transition can be compared to changing the engines on an airliner while the plane is flying. Inasmuch as Kodak filed for bankruptcy in January, 2012, we can conclude the transition was unsuccessful.

A thought-provoking perspective on business-model change for technology companies was provided by Ernest von Simson in his book *The Limits of Strategy*. The author postulates that nearly any strategy designed by an incumbent CEO will fail in the face of a disruptive technology because it requires a vastly different business model and a different management discipline as well.[54]

Another example that comes to mind with which I've had personal experience is a large acquisition that involves the issuance of a significant amount of debt. Even though the transaction makes sense in terms of fit and synergy, cost reduction, integrations of systems, melding of cultures, and resolving management issues are time consuming and distracting, and the anticipated increase in shareholder value may not occur or involve years to realize.

While there are always exceptions to generalizations, my experience leads me to conclude that, for whatever reason, when a company whose stock you own is about to undergo fundamental change on a large scale, it may be time to sell or at the very least scale back the size of your investment. And when the changes being contemplated cause investor exuberance and an unsustainable stock price premium, the odds favor selling the entire holding.

Poor Execution of Business Plan

Investors are attracted to a company with a robust strategy and a coherent business plan—and rightly so since they are important ingredients to consider in evaluating investment opportunities. However, the goals and objectives that provide substance to the business plan will become unfulfilled promises if operational execution is sloppy and sporadic. Larry Bossidy, a former executive of General Electric and retired CEO of Allied Signal, describes execution as "the great unaddressed issue in the business world today."[55] He considers absence of effective execution the single biggest obstacle to success and the cause of many problems and disappointments mistakenly attributed to other causes.

In today's fast-moving and highly competitive world, one must anticipate that even the best-managed company will not always meet or exceed every performance metric. However, if overall, a company consistently falls short of many of its key goals and objectives, this is a clear sign that execution is poor and is not a top priority of management. An investor who owns the stock of a company with a poor record of execution should sell the holding. Absent a change in management, inconsistent execution will deliver mediocre or even poor results, making it highly unlikely that a stock investment will prove to be worthwhile in terms of delivering returns exceeding that of the market.

A bright red flag signaling the potential for disappointing execution of a business plan is a merger or acquisition; four out of five fail to deliver anticipated results, and this is especially true for large deals. Acquisitions fall short of expected benefits for many reasons. In a feature article about the giant consumer products company Proctor and Gamble that appeared in the *Economist*, CEO Arthur Lafley offers five reasons why mergers fail.[56] These reasons include poor strategic fit, totally different cultures, incompatible senior management, failure to deliver costs savings, and increased revenues. Additionally, integrating a merger or acquisition is always a distraction—for *at least* a year— creating conditions that can lead to neglecting the core business. Despite the unfavorable odds for success, the hype associated with a proposed merger or acquisition frequently results in a rise in the stock price of the acquiring company. When this occurs, investors are presented with a unique opportunity to objectively assess the situation and sell the stock if the price is reflecting all of the benefits of an acquisition and ignoring all of the risks.

Stock Price Significantly
Higher Than Intrinsic Value

Evaluating and monitoring the intrinsic value of a stock should be a continuing process. I suggest conducing a valuation update quarterly, following the earnings release or whenever management makes an announcement concerning a significant change in the financial outlook for the company. The discipline of periodically revisiting the intrinsic value of the stock of a company forces the investor to determine the extent to which the stock is overvalued or undervalued. Just as equity markets tend to become overvalued at times, individual stocks can rise to a level that is significantly higher than intrinsic or fair value. In this instance, *significantly higher* is defined as more than 50 percent.[57] Assume that the intrinsic value of the stock of a company whose earnings per share have a high probability of growing at the rate of 10 percent annually is seventeen times earnings, but the current price is twenty-five times earnings. If reversion to the mean is a legitimate consideration, it could be as long as four years before future earnings (assuming a consistent 10 percent annual growth rate) support a price-earnings ratio of seventeen. The elapsed period of time represents significant opportunity costs, not to mention the incurred risk of a potential financial performance shortfall.

Reacting to excessively high stock price valuation is not to be considered as an exercise in market timing, but rather an attempt to optimize the risk/reward relationship of an equity portfolio, thereby increasing the odds of generating returns over time that exceed those of an equity index fund.

Source of Cash

In today's investment environment a pure buy-and-hold strategy for common stocks is a mythical concept. A successful investment program produces gains that represent a source of cash that can and deserves to be spent for a variety reasons, such as a new car, a sizeable down payment on a bigger home, income tax payments, a special vacation, or a major charitable contribution. The examples just mentioned are not mandatory expenditures (with the possible exception of taxes) and might not be possible if one strictly adhered to a buy-and-hold strategy. For those of us who have an IRA, account distributions become mandatory at age seventy, and postponing the sale of securities is not an option. Any time cash reserves are increased or there is a need to distribute cash in excess of existing reserves, there is an implied requirement to sell shares of stocks owned in the portfolio.

Having determined that circumstances will dictate the sale of a stock at some point, it behooves investors to develop a decision process that will result in identifying the best sale candidates. A timely sale is the antithesis of a timely purchase. Ideally a sale candidate should be in favor and selling at a price considerably higher than its intrinsic value. Just as one should not expect to buy a stock at its low, picking the high point for a sale is unlikely. Knowing when or at what level to sell is a challenging aspect of managing an individual portfolio; however, the reality is that individual investors must face up to the challenge and develop the skills and judgment required to achieve maximum positive impact.

Chapter Summary

- Knowing when to sell a stock is one of the most challenging aspects of individual investing.

- In today's environment a buy-and-hold strategy for common stocks is likely to result in investment returns no better than what can be achieved with index funds.

- There are a number of reasons why a stock should be sold, and they include a wrong decision regarding purchase; a change in a company's business model; poor execution of the business plan; a stock price that has risen to a level much higher than intrinsic value; and the need for additional cash.

- Selling has become a legitimate phase of the investment process.

CHAPTER THIRTEEN
Required Mind-Set for Success

One approach to determining the attributes required for investment success is to examine the characteristics and attributes of investors who have demonstrated superior performance over a period of many years. Another approach is to reflect on the thinking process that an individual— take me, for instance—has used over a period of time that appears to have contributed to or detracted from investment success.

While I cannot claim to have conducted an exhaustive analysis of scores of consistently successful investors, I've read enough to gain an appreciation for some of the common threads that help explain how they approach their profession and what guides their decision making. I have had more successes than mistakes, but I have learned from both—maybe learning even more from painful mistakes. It's with the benefit of what I've observed and learned about the attributes of others, along with my own idea of what's important based on personal experience, that I propose a set of attributes that comprise the required mind-set for investment success.

A Strong Value Bias

What seems to be one of the most prevalent attributes of successful investors is the intense concern for buying a stock when the price is selling at a discount to fair or intrinsic value. In simple terms professional investors can be slotted in one of three categories: value investors, growth investors, or eclectic investors (a combination of growth and value). While stock selection criteria will vary by category, all three types of investors will have developed a valuation framework with which to guide purchase price decisions. Generally speaking, price limits will reflect a determination to buy a stock below its fair value so as to improve the odds for an above-average return and provide a margin of safety with which to offset the risks of uncertainties.

A bias for value explains why some successful investors are attracted to stocks that are out of favor, unrecognized, or, for whatever reason, being ignored. Buying at a discount involves accepting the trade-off of uncertainty and lack of visibility. There are also times when a stock sells at a discount because of a major correction in the stock market rather than for company-specific reasons. In any event, before a stock is purchased an investor should determine its intrinsic value and then make a judgment regarding what constitutes an appropriate discount. Some successful investors insist on buying a stock only when its price is selling 30 percent or more below its intrinsic value.

Obviously, one of the important steps is calculating the intrinsic value. This can be accomplished in a number of ways, ranging from a simple price-earnings ratio calculation to a comprehensive discounted cash flow (DCF) analysis. In practice most investors will use more than one methodology, including a discounted cash flow analysis, and then, through the application of judgment and common sense, arrive at a conclusion. All approaches require the investor to make assumptions, and it's important to avoid being overly optimistic.

Independence

It is apparent that investors with a consistent record of success are independent thinkers. It is essential for an individual investor to avoid being carried away by the mood of the crowd, a task that is not easy to accomplish. In 1896 a French philosopher by the name of Dr. Gustave

Le Bon wrote what remains one of the most important works on mass psychology. One of the conclusions he reached about a crowd was the following: "Whoever be the individuals that compose it, however like or unlike be their mode of life, their occupations, their character, or their intelligence, the fact that they have been transformed into a crowd puts them in possession of a sort of collective mind which makes them feel, think, and act in a manner quite different from that in which each individual of them would feel, think, and act were he in a state of isolation." Le Bon also concluded that a striking feature of the crowd is having great difficulty in separating the imagined from the real and distinguishing between the objective and subjective. Other unique characteristics of crowds, he stated, include impulsiveness, incapacity to reason, absence of judgment, and exaggeration of sentiments—a near blindness to the truth.

If one is prepared to accept Le Bon's observations, it is not a stretch to conclude that individuals capable of conducting an objective analysis of a company are in a much better position to select stocks with above-average return potential than they would if purchasing from a list of candidates that represented consensus thinking or stocks currently in vogue. Given the characteristics of the crowd, it is my belief that for an individual investor to realize returns exceeding those of the market or an index fund, he or she must develop and consistently apply independent thinking. An unwillingness or inability to take an independent stand is a precursor to disappointing investment results.

Discipline and Patience

Every successful investor has his or her own style and philosophy. What seems to be a critical element in compiling a successful track record is adhering to one's chosen philosophy and the consistent application of a decision framework. Consistent adherence is not easy; it requires discipline, perseverance, and patience. There will be times when a stock chosen for the portfolio does not appear to be working out or investors choose not to assign a higher valuation even though it is warranted because of good performance.

One should establish a research methodology and stick to it. A disciplined and systematic analysis will not guarantee the elimination of mistakes, but it should lead to better and more timely stock selection, thereby improving long-term returns. Owning only a few different stocks at one time makes it possible to develop a comprehensive understanding of each company represented in the portfolio. A complete understanding of the company and its environment, strengths, and weaknesses should improve the odds of selecting good companies at attractive prices. Here, again, discipline is required to limit the portfolio to the companies with the best long-term prospects.

Stock prices are always in a state of flux. Prices levels change from one hour to the next, and the volatility is often in response to investor emotions stimulated by rumors, technical patterns, news items, and new expectations based on actual operating results. Successful investing, therefore, requires a focus on realism, a disposition to think and act objectively and unemotionally. My own experience has provided me with insights regarding the relative ease with which overly optimistic assumptions can overshadow the risks and uncertainties inherent in common stock ownership. It's important not to get carried away in assessing the outlook of a particular company. Recognize that even the most exciting opportunity will not play out smoothly or without setbacks. Realistically examining the facts and conservatively assessing the prospects of a company requires mental discipline and a willingness to reject or downplay popular thinking.

Patience involves a willingness to wait for price to reflect the reality of improving fundamentals. It may take a while for investors to not only recognize but develop confidence in an improving situation. However, investors should not be patient when it comes to the expectation of improving fundamentals and financial performance. If management is slow to address problems or chooses to ignore them, this should be a source of significant concern—and perhaps the basis for rejecting an investment opportunity or selling a stock in one's portfolio.

A Desire for Simplicity

The proposed attribute of simplicity is a more recently developed insight prompted by an investor who has demonstrated extraordinary performance. An institutional investor named Mohnish Pabrai compounded money at the rate of 29 percent annually for eight years in his investment partnership. Pabrai believes that two or three very important variables are usually what determine the success or failure of a company; the others are just noise. Pabrai's belief can be viewed as an admonition regarding the pitfalls of information overload and failing to understand what really matters in a company. Many investors— professional as well as individual—risk getting bogged down in the minutiae and details of a company, thereby missing the big things that make or break the investment. Sophisticated computer models and dozens of spreadsheets may be very helpful in evaluating corporate performance but are of little or no value in applying the judgment required to select the right stock for purchase.

The purpose of simplification is not to deny the existence of complexity; rather it is to develop approaches that will assist in dealing with an increasingly complex environment, separating the critical from the important and the important from the trivial. We have today, more than ever before, an explosion of information, and the sources and volume of information will continue to grow exponentially. Restricting the number of issues owned at any one time and focusing on the critical variables represent ways to ensure the more effective use of time in analyzing investments and achieving better results. Former associate director of research at Morgan Stanley, James J. Valentine, CFA, made the point that great analysts distinguish themselves by spending a disproportionate amount of time on evaluating and forecasting a very limited number of factors likely to move a stock.[58]

The observations of Pabrai are consistent with the Perato Principle and the age-old 80/20 Rule, which is to suggest that in any endeavor, the vast majority of results can be attributed to a small percentage of the activities.[59] Use traditional retailing as an example. The critical variable of same-store sales driven by size of transaction and transaction frequency are critical variables of both short- and long-term performance. Selecting a retail company as an investment involves the examination and subsequent monitoring of the initiatives influencing same-store sales. It is possible for a retail company to show growth in revenues by adding stores, but if same-store sales continue to decline, there will ultimately be a day of reckoning.

The idea of striving for simplicity is not new, nor is it restricted to business and investments. In conducting research for material used in this chapter, I came across a rather startling pronouncement by Albert Einstein who listed the five ascending levels of intellect in this order: smart, intelligent, brilliant, genius, simple. If simplicity was assigned top priority by an individual noted for successfully exploring the world of nuclear physics, why should it be of less importance to those whose interests lie in the field of investing?

Critical Thinking

In *The Essential Buffett*, author Robert Hagstrom states that one of the reasons for Warren Buffett's success is his unique combination of investment and management expertise. Buffett has considerable hands-on experience owning and managing a variety of companies. He always analyzes the business factors first when contemplating investing in a company.[60] It's from this perspective that I'm suggesting that we consider critical-thinking skills as an important attribute for individuals who aspire to become successful investors; this attribute is similar to that found in successful CEOs, the special cognitive skill set involved in probing, proving, asking the right questions, and anticipating problems.

Professor Michael Scriven, formerly at Harvard University and more recently at the University of California, Berkeley, is one of the most published authors on the subject of critical thinking and has offered a definition of it that speaks to its essential role in business (and, I have concluded, investing). He described critical thinking as: "The skilled, active interpretation and evaluation of observations, communications, information and argumentation as a guide to thought and action." Justin Menkes, in his book *Executive Intelligence*, states that critical-thinking ability determines how skillfully someone gathers, processes, and applies information in order to determine the best way to reach a particular goal or navigate a complex situation.[61] I would submit that relative to investing in common stocks, the higher the skill level in gathering, processing, and applying information, the greater the odds that investment returns will be superior over time.

Justin Menkes also concludes, "In its simplest form, critical thinking in business [again, I would include investing] involves skillfully working out the best answer you can come up with by identifying and using all information that has value for that purpose and resisting irrelevant and unreliable considerations, however tempting that may be."[62] The point being made is this: a high level of executive intelligence as defined by critical thinking is a very important and advantageous attribute for investment success. Although further discussion regarding executive intelligence is beyond the scope of this chapter, it is reassuring to note that according to Menkes, like any set of skills, critical thinking can be learned, practiced, and improved, and training can have considerable and lasting effects. In my opinion, the process of researching and analyzing a company being considered for investment, coupled with the feedback provided by the company's performance after the investment has been made, are important learning opportunities. Experience is usually a good teacher.

Other Observations Regarding Required Attributes

As a way of corroborating the attributes that have been proposed, I refer to other investors who have shared their points of view regarding the required attributes of success. John Train, a highly successful investment counselor and author, describes in his book *The Money Masters* the methods and investment philosophies of some of the great investors of the twentieth century. He compares the traits of each of these "investment masters" and lists the following:

- He is realistic.

- He is intelligent to the point of genius.

- He is utterly dedicated to his craft.

- He is disciplined and patient.

- He is a loner.[63]

Several of these traits are nearly identical to the list I've developed.

More than forty years ago, a professor by the name of Douglas Bellemore, who had taught investments at New York University for decades and had been an investor for fifty years discussed the traits required for success as an aggressive investor in his book, *The Strategic Investor*.[64] He listed these five as patience, courage, intelligence, emotional stability, and hard work. Bellemore also concluded that not all investors have the innate personal characteristics required to succeed in outperforming the market over time. He went on to mention a sixth attribute, which he described as the "willingness to sacrifice the investment protection of diversification." He supported that requisite with the statement that, while conservative investors rely on diversification to minimize risks, the aggressive investor must forgo wide diversification if a portfolio of stocks is to significantly outperform the general market. I found it interesting that portfolio concentration (the theme of this book) was being advocated nearly half a century ago as a means of achieving superior results.

No commentary on investor attributes would be complete without another reference to Warren Buffett. In the 1992 Berkshire Hathaway annual report, Buffett made the following statement: "What counts for most people in investing is not how much they know, but rather how realistically they define what they don't know. An investor needs to do very few things right as long as he or she avoids big mistakes." Those words say volumes about the importance of a disciplined approach to investing as a requisite for success.

Chapter Summary

- Considerable evidence suggests that successful investors focus on the fair value of a stock and where the price stands in relation to that value at the time of purchase and throughout the period of ownership.

- Although independent thinking is no guarantee of superior investment performance, its absence virtually assures mediocrity.

- Simplify the approach to investing by focusing on the few critical variables that determine success or failure.

CHAPTER FOURTEEN
Sources of Information

———————————

Never before has so much information been available for the individual investor—and most of it can be obtained without charge. The almost unlimited availability is made possible because of the Internet, and with the possible exception of message boards, the quality of the information is also good. But like so many other facets of financial and business activity, the quantity, quality, and timeliness of information is subordinate to good judgment in terms of importance. Relevant data and information may be the foundation for a good decision; however, interpreting the facts, evaluating the critical issues, and weighing the alternatives are the key mental tasks that precede a decision.

In today's environment the potential exists for information overload, a condition that increases the odds of being overwhelmed, unable to distinguish between what is critical and what is just nice to know. What follows is a list of information sources I use and have found to be helpful in understanding companies I've considered for investment. The categories of sources should remain relevant for years to come;

however, in some cases the specific sources may become less useful or may be replaced by something else.

Company Website

Over the past several years virtually every publicly owned company has developed a website; and almost without exception every company website has a corporate and investor relations section. The corporate section presents information about products and services, corporate press releases, details about executive management, and a brief history of the company. The investor relations section typically will provide access to annual and quarterly reports, the annual proxy statement, financial press releases, analyst coverage, SEC filings, conference calls, corporate governance, and in some cases earnings estimates made by brokerage firms. The company website is an excellent information source with which to begin the process of researching a potential investment.

Other Websites

There are many other sources of information available on Internet sites. I have found money.msn.com easy to use and quite comprehensive in terms of content (it's also free). Standard available information for each company includes company financials, a summary of the company's business, share ownership information, earnings estimates, price charts, and a link to the company website.

The NASDAQ website is also a convenient source of information and provides access to summary information on stock price, company financials, price charts, as well as a link to the SEC website, along with company press releases and other relevant information.

One of the most productive sources of information for me, which just became available within the past two years, is the Magic Formula website developed in conjunction with *The Little Book That Beats The Market*, written by Joel Greenblatt, successful investor and adjunct professor at Columbia Business School. Currently, the website can be accessed without charge and conveniently identifies good companies selling at attractive prices relative to each company's historical earnings and return on investment.[65] The website is updated daily, as the list of stocks identified as the most attractive (limited to a maximum of one hundred names) is sensitive to price. I usually visit the website several times every month to stay current and uncover which additional companies I should research as candidates for my portfolio.

Every investor who is conducting research on a specific company should use the Google search engine at some point. I usually enter the name of the company and see what is produced. Using Google to gather information about senior management, products, competitors, and miscellaneous corporate activities can also be useful.

SEC Documents

The SEC website is a necessary resource. A company's annual filing of the Form 10-K and Proxy statement and quarterly filing of the 10-Q are mandatory, and referring to them prior to investing in the company is essential. Investors who choose not to download those documents may contact the company for printed versions, although that involves delays due to handling and mailing. From time to time a company will release other important information, and typically this information is filed with the SEC on a Form 8-K, which can also be accessed by investors.

Company Conference Calls

The Internet makes it possible for a company to host conference calls, and it has become commonplace for most publicly owned corporations—large and small—to schedule a call once every quarter in connection with the release of interim earnings. The chief executive officer and the chief financial officer typically participate on the call, and sometimes other executives are present as well, such as the executive in charge of sales or marketing. The conference call normally begins with prepared remarks from the CEO and CFO, followed by a question-and-answer session, which is what I find most interesting. Investment analysts from the research departments of prominent brokerage firms typically participate via telephone. They are usually well informed about the company and the industry and are in a position to ask pertinent questions. Management is somewhat constrained with regard to providing answers; however, the interchange that takes place usually provides some important insights regarding the results for the quarter and the near-term outlook.

On occasion a company will be asked to participate in an industry conference sponsored by a brokerage firm. Many times the featured companies will webcast their presentation, making it possible for shareholders and prospective investors to listen in.

Brokerage Services

Many Wall Street brokerage firms provide services to their customers in addition to the execution of buy and sell orders. There are discount brokers and full-service brokers; I use one of each. My discount broker happens to be Fidelity, so I will use them as an example of what services are available to an individual investor. The commission rate for executing a buy or sell trade online is a maximum of $19.95 per trade for the first 1,000 shares and $0.015 per share thereafter. Trading with the assistance of a Fidelity representative involves a higher commission rate. The online commission rate for large accounts (assets in excess of $1 million) is $8.00 per trade regardless of the number of shares. Other discount brokers charge comparable commission rates.

Fidelity offers a broad array of services besides trading. Record-keeping capability is extensive and makes it possible for an individual investor to instantly monitor trades and see all capital gains and losses. Research reports are available online for most publicly owned companies, and a screening device can be used to identify stocks that meet certain criteria. Reports from First Call that display earnings estimates can also be accessed online. While the available information varies by company, it is generally sufficient to make an informed judgment regarding the investment merits of a particular company and whether or not to proceed with all of the research necessary to purchase the stock.

Purchased Services

In addition to the many free sources of information, there are also proprietary information services that can be obtained for a fee. I have subscribed to the basic service of Value Line for many years and find it useful for gathering historical information (available for about 1,800 publicly traded companies). Each company covered is summarized on one page, which includes a price chart. Value Line offers a number of additional services covering smaller companies. The services are available in either printed reports or online, and current prices for services run about several hundred dollars annually depending on which ones are used.

Morningstar offers a number of research products including a service specifically designed for individual investors. The Select Equity Research service includes reports on over 1,800 companies; analyst access via phone and e-mail; interactive discounted cash flow models; and e-mail alerts and updates. This service can be obtained for about $150 per year.

Periodicals

If one were to read only one financial publication, it would have to be the *Wall Street Journal*. I subscribe to both the *Wall Street Journal* and *Barron's* online and to printed versions of *Business Week* and *Fortune*. These publications provide timely information and context relating to companies and industries. I would also recommend a subscription to the *Economist*, a magazine that is international in scope and has a section devoted to business as well as finance and economics. The magazine also contains articles on a broad array of valuable topics that help to provide context for investors. The editorial offices are in London, and the magazine was first published in 1843.

The *Harvard Business Review*, while not specifically written for investors, does provide information related to corporate strategy, management principles, marketing, and a host of other business-related topics. The magazine may not generate a specific candidate for an investor's portfolio but can prove useful in providing a benchmark against which to compare the performance, competitive strength, and investment attractiveness of a given company.

Management Visits

Once an investor has completed his or her homework on a company, there might be a need to visit with a company representative in order to have a few issues clarified or questions answered. Today, most companies, regardless of size, have an investor relations department or representative whose function is to interact with shareholders and prospective investors. My experience with investor relations representatives has been positive for the most part; they are well informed and usually articulate, as well. However, it's important for the investor to have done his or her homework before making a call. On rare occasions I may personally visit a particular company and its representative, but most often I will call to schedule a telephone interview. During that initial call I promise to send an e-mail providing information on my background and investment experience and a list of specific questions to guide the interview process. Without exception my lists of questions have been appreciated since they provided focus and made for efficient use of time.

Regarding the actual interview with a management representative, be aware of the legal constraint imposed on management of publicly owned companies by way of SEC Regulation FD, which became effective in October of 2000. The rule is designed to eliminate selective disclosure of material nonpublic information and promote full and fair disclosure of information by the management of publicly owned companies. There are specific examples of what a company management or its representative will not do, which includes commenting on earnings estimates or financial models. However, the SEC does not want to discourage investors and analysts from asking questions or visiting with management. The following statement was extracted from the language describing Regulation FD and is intended to provide relevant context for investors as they engage in dialogue with company representatives:

At the same time, an issuer is not prohibited from disclosing a non-material piece of information to an analyst, even if, unbeknownst to the issuer, that piece helps the analyst complete a "mosaic" of information that, taken together, is material. Similarly, since materiality is an objective test keyed to the reasonable investor,

Regulation FD will not be implicated where an issuer discloses immaterial information whose significance is discerned by the analyst. Analysts can provide a valuable service in sifting through and extracting information that would not be significant to the ordinary investor to reach material conclusions. We do not intend, by Regulation FD, to discourage this sort of activity. The focus of Regulation FD is on whether the issuer discloses material nonpublic information, not on whether an analyst, through some combination of persistence, knowledge, and insight, regards as material information whose significance is not apparent to the reasonable investor.

A personal visit to a company headquarters is usually interesting and may be slightly more informative than a visit by telephone. However, from a practical standpoint the added value is not likely to justify the cost of an airline ticket, meals, and hotel room, especially if the size of the holding is small.

Other Sources of Information and Ideas

Every investor who has a natural curiosity has an important advantage. Curiosity is an attribute that will cause a person to contemplate the investment merits of a company offering products and/or services that one buys, uses, or sees in stores or advertised in the media. I have heard about individual investors who are very unsophisticated about finance and investing but have been very successful through buying and holding on to stocks of companies in which they had a great deal of confidence because they used and liked their products. The stocks of consumer goods companies and retailers are examples of potential investments that can be evaluated from the standpoint of the investor as a customer. If one likes something as a customer, why not evaluate the company as an investment opportunity? On the other hand if one is dissatisfied with a product or service and encounters other people who feel the same way, perhaps that's a warning to avoid the company as an investment.

Collecting and reading business books written by knowledgeable and thought-provoking authors is a favorite activity of mine, and it has served me well as I consider companies for my investment portfolio.

For example, I've read many of the books written by Peter Drucker, who in the opinion of some was considerably ahead of his time in understanding the critical ingredients of business success. One of the first books I acquired after graduate school was Peter Drucker's *Managing for Results*, written in 1964, nearly fifty years ago. In the first chapter of that book Drucker listed a number of business realities including that "economic results are earned only by leadership" and that "any leadership position is transitory and likely to be short-lived." Ultimately, economic results drive long-term investment performance, and it is hard to identify other realities that deserve more scrutiny than the manner in which a company is providing leadership in something of real and lasting value to a customer or market.[66] That reality has stood the test of time and is even more relevant today than when the book was written.

I have many investment books in my library and usually add two or three books every year about successful investors like Warren Buffett or written by successful investors like Phil Fisher or Benjamin Graham. Most of these books do not offer specific investment ideas, but rather stimulate thinking about what to look for that will improve the odds for above-average investment gains. Of all of the investment books I've acquired and read, my favorite is probably *Common Stocks and Uncommon Profits* by Philip Fisher. Although I consider myself to be very sensitive to valuation when taking a position in a stock, Fisher's investment philosophy embraces both the quantitative and qualitative dimensions of investing, which I believe are as important as ever.

Finally one cannot overlook an obvious source of information and ideas: friends, acquaintances, and other investors. I'm not suggesting that hot tips should be the basis for selecting stocks; however, if someone tells you about an investment opportunity and provides a strong rationale regarding its merits, you should not discard the idea out of hand. Given the abundance of information that's been described in this chapter, it shouldn't take long to take a preliminary look using the criteria that have been outlined in this book and make a determination as to whether or not to complete your research and perhaps purchase a particular stock for your portfolio.

Chapter Summary

- There is more investment information available for individual investors than ever before, and much of it is available without charge.

- A company's website is the place to begin the search for information while you are evaluating the company's stock for investment.

- The Securities and Exchange Commission (SEC) website is a resource available to the investing public that provides access to important documents, including the annual Form 10-K and quarterly Form 10-Q for every publicly held company traded on a US exchange.

- Company conference calls, usually conducted quarterly, are a valuable resource and now can be accessed via the Internet for virtually all publicly owned companies. Many, if not most, companies will grant interviews to individual investors.

- Periodicals, books on business and investments, and personal contacts are valuable sources of information and ideas regarding investment strategy and specific stocks.

CHAPTER 15
Financial Market Reality

F̲ollowing the completion of my graduate studies at Northwestern University (at what is now the Kellogg School of Management) I went to work for the St. Paul Fire and Marine Insurance Company (now part of Travelers) as an investment analyst. My initial assignment involved analyzing municipal bonds, and I later was given responsibility for analyzing common stocks. Sometime after this reassignment, I was asked to make a presentation to a group of company officers on the subject of trends in investment management. In preparing my remarks for the meeting, I gained a better understanding of the changes that were underway in financial markets and later concluded that the 1960s marked the beginning of a period of accelerating change in equity markets. As the institutionalization of money management grew during those years, investors saw the emergence of professional research of common stocks, negotiated commissions, block trading, and a much greater emphasis on investment performance. As an interesting aside to these changes, the Dow Jones Industrial Average was virtually flat from 1965 through 1980, reaching and only briefly exceeding 1,000 on several occasions but never truly going beyond that level until 1981. As the saying goes, change is a constant, and that has been especially true with regard to financial markets generally and equity markets in particular. What follows is a description of some substantive changes that have occurred since the 1960s.

Growth in Derivatives

Derivatives are specialized contracts which contain an agreement or an option to buy or sell an underlying asset up to a certain time in the future at a prearranged price (the exercise price). The history of derivatives goes back further than most people think. Evidence of derivative contracts can even be found that date back to the ages before Christ. However, the advent of modern-day derivative contracts is attributed to the need for farmers to protect themselves from any decline in the price of their crops due to delayed monsoon or to overproduction. The Chicago Board of Trade (CBOT), the largest derivative exchange in the world, was established in 1848 and standardized forward contracts on various commodities around 1865. From then on, futures contracts have remained more or less in the same form that we know today.

The new era for the derivative markets was ushered in with the introduction of financial derivatives in the 1970s, and it continues to this day. Although commodity derivatives, particularly oil and precious metals, are still quite active, financial derivatives dominate trading in the current derivative markets. Alan Greenspan, former chairman of the US Federal Reserve, considers the extraordinary development and expansion of financial derivatives to be the most significant event in finance during the past decade. He believes these instruments enhance the ability to differentiate risk and allocate it to those investors most able and willing to take it on. Derivatives were designed to contain risk; however, trading in derivatives is very complicated and can be risky since a small percentage change in the underlying asset can cause a much larger percentage change in the price of the derivative.

Derivatives are an innovation that has redefined the financial services industry, and they have assumed a very significant place in the capital markets. Although the United States remains the dominant market, derivatives have become an important instrument in global finance. Put and call options are an important segment of the financial derivative market; their existence and widespread use represents yet another layer of complexity that impacts the price of individual stocks and the overall equity market.

Growth of Hedge Funds

A hedge fund is a private investment fund that charges a performance fee and is typically open to only a limited range of qualified investors. Hedge fund activity in the global securities markets has grown substantially. Hedge funds dominate certain specialty markets such as trading in derivatives with high-yield ratings, and distressed debt. Total assets of hedge funds on a global basis exceeded $2 trillion at the beginning of 2011.

As the name implies, hedge funds often seek to offset potential losses in the principal markets that they invest in by hedging via any number of methods. However, the term *hedge fund* has come to be overused and inappropriately applied to any absolute-return fund; many of these so-called hedge funds do not actually hedge their investments. Because reporting requirements placed on hedge funds are less onerous than those for traditional mutual funds, they are more secretive, and reporting to investors is much less transparent. Hedge fund managers are very aggressive. Because of their size, use of leverage, willingness to take risk, and ability to go long or short, hedge funds can significantly move the price of a stock up or down in a very short period of time. Hedge fund management has also developed the reputation of being very assertive at times with the management of companies owned in the portfolio—especially when there's evidence that shareholder value needs to be unlocked.

The growth of hedge funds in recent years and the scope and size of their trading activity strongly suggests that this class of investors is contributing to higher volatility in the market, and their actions may not always be consistent with changes in the outlook for the companies whose stocks are being bought and sold. You can be sure that, as a company's earnings for a particular quarter are reported and the earnings are either above or below the consensus, one or more hedge funds will attempt to capitalize on the surprise. Thus, price movements of 5 percent or more in a single day are no longer unusual, even for companies with large market capitalizations. Hedge funds are here to stay, but the industry is currently reinventing itself and adopting best practices to address sweeping regulatory changes and investor demands for enhanced fund transparency, liquidity and efficiency. These changes, however, are not likely to change the aggressive style of hedge fund managers. Therefore, individual investors must learn to operate in the existing environment and capitalize on whatever opportunities are presented, remembering that volatility should be considered a friend.

Globalization of Financial Markets

There is no doubt that world financial markets are moving rapidly towards globalization, along with the integration of local financial markets to international financial systems and institutions. The globalization phenomenon may be a blessing that enhances national economies, or it may increase pricing volatility and trading instability when, for instance, irrational trading or crises in one market or region move to other markets and regions as we have witnessed in the last two decades.

In a keynote address at the Cato Institute's Fifteenth Annual Monetary Conference in 1997, Alan Greenspan, former chairman of the Federal Reserve, discussed the globalization of finance. He attributed the dramatic expansion of cross-border financial flows to the rapid increase in telecommunications and computer-based technologies and products. He stated that world financial markets are far more efficient than ever before and that the new instruments and risk-management techniques made possible by technology have enabled an ever-wider range of firms to manage financial risks more effectively. However, Mr. Greenspan also identified new challenges facing central bankers, markets, and market participants; for example, a disturbance in one market segment or one country is likely to be transmitted far more rapidly throughout the world economy than in previous eras. He also identified the need for central banks to address the inevitable increase in systemic risk and recognize that the present efficiency of global markets can transmit mistakes at a pace far greater than ever before. In his closing statement he reminded attendees that the rapidly changing global financial system must retain the capacity to contain market shocks since their occurrence is inevitable.[67]

Ten years later, Mr. Greenspan devoted many pages of his book *The Age of Turbulence* to the topic of globalization. He wrote, "The resulting advance of global financial markets has markedly improved the efficiency with which the world's savings are invested, a vital indirect contributor to world productivity growth. As I saw it, from 1995 forward, the largely unregulated global markets, with some notable exceptions, appeared to be moving smoothly from one state of equilibrium to another."[68] It seems reasonable to conclude, therefore, that globalization of financial markets has continued and world equity markets are linked. Early 2008 provided numerous examples of how a marked decline in stock prices in the United States could be immediately followed by a significant decline in stock prices in both Asian and European markets. Notwithstanding the significant progress of the past ten to twenty years, one should still assume there will be times when stock prices, at least in the short run, will be impacted by developments abroad.

Once again we can state that the individual investor is not in a position to influence events of a global nature. With technology as a primary catalyst, change in global financial markets will continue, and volatility in prices is a likely by-product. Therefore, individual investors must adapt, learn to live with the changes, and take advantage of whatever opportunities present themselves—and there will be many.

Computerized Trading

Technology has impacted stock trading as well. A 2007 article in *BusinessWeek* mentions a sea change in trading.[69] "'The days when humans traded with each other are gone. Now computers trade with each other,' says James Angel, associate professor of finance at Georgetown University's McDonough School of Business. 'Computerized systems are capable of handling big spikes in volume with minimal problems.'" The article goes on to describe how the market is now able to execute trades through online brokers or institutional investors using algorithms and electronic trading systems to place orders.

One application of computerized trading is program trading. In general terms, program trading is when computer algorithms automatically trigger trades in response to market signals, such as price changes in a given stock. According to the New York Stock Exchange, program trading during 2006 and 2007 ranged from a weekly low of

25 percent to a high of 50 percent, with an average week standing at close to 30 percent. On some days stock prices will move significantly in a matter of minutes, and frequently the price changes can be traced to programmed trading activity.

Then there are the traders with the black boxes in Lower Manhattan and Greenwich, Connecticut, who have written ultrasecret algorithms that dictate the purchase or sale of stocks whenever prices hit certain levels. In the past few years, quantitatively driven hedge funds have proliferated. And every day, the code on which they rely can trigger a buy and a sell on the same groups of stocks—sometimes several times a day. Thanks to program trading, a relatively small quantitative firm with only several hundred million dollars in capital can nonetheless account for a big chunk of the daily volume on the New York Stock Exchange.

Computerized trading appears to have contributed to an increased volatility in the price of common stocks, which can confuse and frustrate the efforts of individual investors. However, little can be done to counteract this reality except for each investor to be in a position to take advantage of sudden drops in the prices of stocks that have been identified as candidates for purchase. Volatility, seen from that point of view, can be considered an opportunity to enhance the investment return of a portfolio.

Behavioral Finance

For several decades the conventional wisdom of many if not the majority of sophisticated investors held that the pricing of common stocks was efficient, that is, at any point in time the stock price of a company reflected all of the known and relevant information about it. This conventional wisdom, referred to as the Efficient Market Hypothesis (EMH), evolved in the 1960s from the PhD dissertation of an academic named Eugene Fama. He made the persuasive argument that in an active market of many well-informed and intelligent investors, securities will be appropriately priced and reflect all available information. Critics of EMH argue that stock return prices also reflect the psychological factors, social movements, noise trading, and fashions or fads of irrational investors, all of which come under the heading of behavioral finance. Many researchers believe the study of psychology and other social sciences can shed considerable light on the efficiency of financial markets as well as explain many stock market anomalies, market bubbles, and crashes, and that these human flaws are consistent, predictable, and can be exploited for profit.

An investor by the name of James Montier, who has studied and written extensively about behavioral finance, has concluded that real-world investors are not always rational. He discusses some of the common behavioral traits that underlie irrational thinking and biases of judgment including over-optimism; overconfidence; cognitive dissonance (the mental conflict people experience when solid evidence indicates that beliefs or assumptions are wrong); confirmation bias (a desire to find information that corroborates an existing point of view; and conservatism bias (the tendency to cling tenaciously to a point of view or forecast).[70]

Notwithstanding the arguments of those who believe in market efficiency, Montier demonstrates that mistakes in judgment made by investors are not the random blips of efficient markets, but rather the persistent and, to some extent, predictable outcomes attributable to the psychological biases identified above and inherent in most investors. And if one believes these biases can significantly impact stock prices, then recognizing them and ascertaining the degree of their impact can provide investors with the opportunity to buy or sell a stock when its price is temporarily below or above fair value. The manifestations of behavioral finance include potential price volatility, but as we've discussed elsewhere, volatility needs to be viewed as a friend since it's capable of creating bargain opportunities for an investment portfolio. What could be more appealing to a potential investor than a stock whose price has been temporarily inflated or depressed for reasons that have little to do with the fundamentals of the business?

The Trading Mentality

As one contemplates the significant changes that have occurred in financial markets over the past two to three decades, especially as they involve derivatives, hedge funds, globalization, computerized trading, and behavioral finance, it should come as no surprise that a trading mentality has developed that is unlikely to disappear; actually, it may even intensify. Time horizons vary, of course, from one group of investors to the next. There are professionals whose job it is to make a market in a stock and as a result trade it many times each day. We have day traders along with individuals or institutions who will take a position in a given stock, expecting to trade for a few points. The track record of some mutual fund managers reflects turnover of 100 percent over twelve months. Even value investors trade by purchasing a stock at a discount to fair value and then selling it once a target price (presumably fair value) is reached. Electronic trading, low commissions, and market liquidity have contributed to this trading environment.

Of recent concern is the power of very large traders, such as the major hedge funds who have a short-term focus. In a recent *New York Times* article, Ben Stein describes the ability of the huge traders, who can sell massive amounts of stocks, to move prices and the market up and down at will.[71] They are capable of overwhelming the market, at least for a while and at any time they want. Depending on their disposition, these traders can create extreme optimism or pessimism for individual stocks and the stock market among investors and throughout the country, almost at the drop of a hat and, in Stein's words, "make governments tremble and give central bankers colitis." These traders cause an unsettling environment to exist for the individual investor and can wield immense power by influencing the opinion and actions of journalists, regulators, and politicians.

Trading by investors and speculators is a fact of life. Since 1970, volume on the New York Stock Exchange has increased from an average of 12 million shares per day to 4.8 billion shares per day in 2007; that is a 400-fold increase in trading volume in the span of thirty-seven years. And who knows what the volume will be ten years from now? There can be little doubt, however, that it will be higher, and perhaps significantly so. The impact of trading activity on volatility can be significant, which, in turn, can be devastating to the amateur and discouraging to the experienced individual investor. However, stocks of good companies purchased at a discount to fair value will deliver above-average returns and overshadow the disappointment of a decline in price immediately following purchase, should that occur.

Implications for the Individual Investor

These individual and collective changes represent challenges and opportunities for the individual investor. Many of these changes cause volatility in the price of individual stocks and contribute to heightened investor uncertainty. In turn, increased volatility and uncertainty often result in damaging investor psychology and weakening resolve regarding the implementation of a previously determined course of action. How can the individual investor cope in this more volatile, unpredictable, highly charged, and fast-moving environment? In my opinion the answers to that question are straightforward and consistent with statements made throughout this book:

- Accept the validity of reversion to the mean. What goes up will come down, and what goes down will come up. This idea may not apply to stocks of companies that are in danger of going out of business; but for most other situations it is relevant, and the challenge is to determine at what point the stock of a good company is selling at a significant discount to its fair or intrinsic value.

- Constantly remind yourself that the value of a firm is the sum of future net cash flows discounted at a rate equal to the cost of capital. This theory of valuation has withstood the test of time, and while there are many underlying assumptions, the basic conclusion is that superior financial performance will ultimately be reflected in shareholder value and investor return. Frequently the price of a company's stock fluctuates much more than its fair value.

- Purchase the stock of a good company only when the price is at a significant discount to fair value. Effectively executing this rule requires an understanding of the business and its long-term outlook, the strengths and weaknesses of the company, and the translation of underlying fundamentals into fair value of the common stock.

- Remember that volatility is a friend and not the enemy. Volatility is what makes it possible to purchase a good company at a bargain price; it is a by-product of and reaction to uncertainty and/or irrational behavior.

- Finally, exercise patience and perseverance in the pursuit of above-average investment returns. When a stock experiences a several-fold increase over a period of years, an investor is likely to forget about any regrets or disappointments that were felt immediately following purchase; in retrospect, the fact that the price of the stock may have declined a few points after it was bought really doesn't matter.

CHAPTER 16
Putting It All to Work

O ne of the underlying themes of this book is to buy the common stocks of a few good companies at a cheap price. The word *few* has been chosen to convey the idea of a focused or concentrated portfolio. The term *good companies* implies corporations that have both financial and competitive vitality; buying at a cheap price means purchasing a stock at a level significantly below its fair value. This frame of reference is relatively easy to understand; however, effective and consistent execution is another matter, as outcomes are more uncertain. It is with this theme in mind that I developed the following protocol as a way to identify potential candidates for a portfolio, carefully evaluating the underlying fundamentals of a company and its common stock using the tools and concepts developed in the preceding chapters and, finally, making the purchase decision.

The Quick-Scan Technique

As was suggested in the previous chapter, an individual investor will be confronted with many investment ideas over the course of a time—some of them worthy of pursuing and others deserving of almost immediate rejection. It's important, therefore, to have a technique that facilitates a quick evaluation of a possible investment candidate. Time is a precious commodity for anyone, especially for those who have full-time jobs, and there's no reason to spend a lot of time on an investment idea if it does not measure up to some basic criteria or pass the smell test.

Malcolm Gladwell, author of *Blink*, reveals that great decision-makers are not those individuals who can process the most information or spend the most time thinking, but those who have developed the art of "thin-slicing," that is, identifying and quickly evaluating the few factors that matter most from a huge number of variables.[72] Thin-slicing is a form of rapid cognition that involves the subconscious mind's ability to find patterns in situations and behavior based on very narrow slices of experience. I refer to my version of thin-slicing as a quick scan, but the idea is the same—quickly evaluating those factors most relevant with respect to the theme of buying good companies at cheap prices. I propose evaluating the following factors regarding a company and its common stock and then making a judgment about whether or not to proceed with the remaining research and due diligence required before making a decision to invest.

- *Are the company and its common stock currently out of favor?* I answer this question by calculating the percentage decline in the stock from the high to the low for the most recent fifty-two-week period. The threshold test is a decline of 40 percent or more with the current price closer to the low than the high point of the range. This much of a decline is clear evidence that investors have become disenchanted with a company and its stock, perhaps for good reason, and may have driven the stock price to a level that it does not deserve. As has been stated, a stock can be out of favor for many reasons; however, a stock is more likely to be selling below fair value if it's near the low for the year.

- *What is the core business of the company, and is there evidence of market leadership?* Studies have shown that a company is more likely to experience above-average performance if its strategy is focused and consists of a dominant core and closely related adjacencies. Market leadership typically reflects above-average profit margins. Visit a website like MSN Money to review a summary of the company and examine the trend and level of profit margins. If there are no indications of market leadership or if profit margins are declining, below industry average, or unstable, this would not be consistent with the definition of a good company.

- *Is there credible evidence of financial vitality?* There is a comprehensive discussion of this subject in chapter 7. However, in brief, look for a company with positive cash flow, investment returns exceeding the cost of capital, and a relatively low ratio of debt to equity.

- *How does the company stack up relative to the five Expectation Factors?* After reviewing the historical financial information, a summary of the company, the most recent press releases, and the president's letter in the most recent annual report, quickly determine if anything stands out one way or the other. A majority of below-average EF ratings would suggest going no further with the analysis since good companies would typically be rated above average.

- *Is there evidence the common stock of the company may currently be selling below its intrinsic value?* Using data available at First Call, determine whether or not the common stock is selling at a discount to the industry or its market segment using the PEG ratio (price-earnings ratio divided by the five-year expected growth rate) as the measure. The lower the ratio, the cheaper the price.

An experienced investor with access to a computer should be able to answer these questions in less than an hour. Positive answers to all five questions justify proceeding with a complete analysis of the company. To be sure, further analysis may result in rejecting the candidate, but the quick scan will save considerable research time in that it will rule out further consideration of a stock that isn't going to measure up at current prices.

Next Steps in an Evaluation

Once you've given yourself the green light to proceed with a full-scale analysis, there are a number of steps to follow and questions to be answered that should lead to a conclusion about whether to purchase the stock. These steps involve applying the ideas and tools discussed in earlier chapters. While an evaluation could begin in a number of places, my preference is to conduct the research and evaluation in the order laid out below. My reason has to do with how one conclusion might best inform another or provide a conclusion that an investor may regard as a knock-out factor, one that would strongly suggest there's no point in spending more time on the idea.

- *Is the company in a good business?* Warren Buffett said, "When management with a reputation for brilliance tackles a business with a reputation for poor fundamental economics, it is the reputation of the business that remains intact."[73] This statement leads one to the conclusion that good companies compete in industries with favorable business economics and are managed by capable and dedicated individuals. A relatively quick way to make an assessment of both business conditions and management is to identify companies whose financial performance over a period of several years exhibits above-average profit margins, positive cash flow, and strong balance sheets.

  Another way to evaluate an industry is to examine its structure in terms of the forces that shape competition and profitability. The major forces include the bargaining power of customers as well as suppliers, the threat of substitute products or services, the threat of new entrants, and the degree of rivalry among existing competitors. If these forces are especially intense, almost no company will demonstrate attractive returns; this suggests an uphill battle for any stock even if it appears to be undervalued. Of special concern are the forces of threat of entry and rivalry among existing competitors, both of which limit the profit potential of a company owing to ongoing pricing pressures and the inability to offset rising costs, which in many cases are incurred to improve competitive position.[74]

- *Is the company's chosen strategy right for the times, and can it be implemented using the current business model?* Even though the economics of an industry may be attractive, competitive success is never guaranteed and may be compromised or unachievable because of an inefficient or outdated business model. Wal-Mart replaced Sears as the dominant retailer because of a better business model. Netflix has challenged Blockbuster because of a better business model. Online retailing is gaining market share because of the business model. One important measure regarding the vitality and success of a business model is relative profit margins. The companies with the highest margins in a given industry have an edge, and the reason may well be that those companies have a business model capable of delivering a better value proposition in the minds of the customer.

- *Is the company a leader in providing something that is of real value in the eyes of the customer?* Market leadership, discussed in chapter 14 (and here remembering the writings of Peter Drucker), does not mean that a company needs to be the largest in its industry or first in every product line. Often, being second or third in size makes it possible for a company to concentrate on one segment of the market, a particular class of customer, service, or distribution. That special focus will often result in genuine and sustainable leadership. Without some form of leadership, however, a company is destined to become marginal, and in today's highly competitive environment, marginal performers are incapable of long-term survival. Moreover, leadership positions tend to be short lived, and if leadership in some area is not renewed, mediocrity and marginal performance will follow.

- *Are the quality and depth of the leadership team adequate to achieve or exceed the desired corporate goals and objectives?* Chapter 4 emphasizes the need for competent leadership and management. One approach to assessing the quality of management is to develop an overall Expectation Factor rating. A score below 30 or a rating of 1 for one or more of the five attributes is a warning sign that management does not measure up.

- *Does the company meet all of the tests of financial vitality?* Chapter 7 discusses the importance of financial vitality and describes various metrics to be applied in assessing financial strength. The most reliable and comprehensive indicators of financial vitality are the ratio of debt to total capital (the lower the better) and return on capital (the higher the better). Good companies are financially strong. Given a choice between two companies that are out of favor—one that is financially strong and one that is not—always choose the company with the strong balance sheet.

- *What is the Expectation Factor?* This measure captures five important attributes that have an important influence on the valuation of a common stock. Companies with a total score of less than 30 may not meet the test of a good company. Be especially wary of a company when one or more of the attributes has a rating of 1.

- *Using reasonable assumptions, what are realistic one-year and three-year target prices for the common stock?* Price targets are educated guesses at best; however, they represent an important step in quantifying the potential total return opportunity. Historical price-earnings ratios, relative price-earnings ratios, price-earnings to growth ratios (PEG), and discounted cash flow of future financial performance are some of the ways of establishing price targets. I also use a modified valuation model first introduced by Benjamin Graham that is based on the estimated future growth rate of earnings per share and long-term interest rates.[75]

- *Is the current price below fair value, and does the price of the stock have the potential to at least double in three to four years?* Owning only a few stocks offers an individual investor the luxury of waiting to buy at the right price, meaning a price below fair value. Buying only when the opportunity for gain is significant is critical if one hopes to outperform an index fund. The potential to experience a doubling (or more) in the price of a stock represents a significant gain.

- *What are the critical few variables that will determine the success the company?* Keeping things simple is good advice regardless of the situation; however, that is easier said than done in today's corporate world and environment. Nonetheless, the Pareto Principle (or 80/20 Rule) is alive and well, which is to say that in most situations 80 percent of the results can be attributed to 20 percent of the activity. Taking this principle a step further leads to the conclusion that a small number of variables will determine the success or failure of a corporation. An investor should identify those variables before committing funds and then monitor them on a continuing basis. If an investor cannot identify the variables, that may be a sign that an investment should not be made.

Asset Allocation

Thus far, I have not discussed asset allocation or what percentage of an investment portfolio should be invested in stocks. A comprehensive discussion of asset allocation is outside the scope of this book; however, the topic is of considerable importance and deserves some comment. First of all, this book is all about identifying and selecting stocks for the portfolio, whether the amount allocated to equities is 10 or 100 percent. Individual investors should consciously determine the extent to which their portfolio will consist of a combination of equities, fixed-income securities, alternative investments, and cash. In general terms the asset mix should be determined by a number of factors including one's age, income needs, other sources of income, ability to tolerate volatility, and peace of mind. Considering those factors objectively will result in a wide range of answers from one individual to the next because of the weight each person places on each factor. If income needs are high and tolerance for risk is low, fixed-income investments will emerge as a high priority. A young investor who has no need for investment income and has a high level of tolerance for volatility is likely to allocate a substantial percentage of invested assets to common stocks. Thus, there is no one answer; it all depends on the situation.

There is an abundance of rules of thumb about asset allocation. For example, many pension and endowment funds will allocate 25 to 30 percent of assets to fixed-income investments and 70 to 75 percent to equity investments. However, in recent years the allocation process has involved specifying in greater detail what should be allocated to alternative investments, foreign securities, emerging markets, and the like. Another rule of thumb for individuals is to own bonds as a percentage of total investments in an amount where the percentage allocation is equal to your age. In other words, a person who is sixty-five years old would have a portfolio where bonds equal 65 percent of the portfolio. I do not happen to agree with the merits of this rule, but some people do. In the final analysis, what is being determined is what portion of the portfolio will be invested in securities with a fixed return, how much will be invested in securities with a variable return, and what the cash position in the portfolio should be. In my own case, my portfolio consists of common stocks and cash (I currently own no bonds); however, I find myself beginning to own good companies that are paying quarterly dividends and have a record of increasing them on a regular basis. Focusing on dividend-paying stocks not only serves to satisfy a portion of one's income needs but is also consistent with the long-term record of dividends representing a significant portion of total investment return.

Finally, we have the subject of cash position to address. As discussed in other parts of this book, anticipating major moves in the stock market has not been a rewarding strategy, and many well-known investors have consistently advised against trying to outguess the market. However, there are times when a cash position will or should increase. For example, investors who own a self-directed IRA and are subject to mandatory distributions should have one to two years of future payout set aside in the form of cash equivalents. Having such a reserve minimizes the risk of having to liquidate securities in an untimely way. A portfolio that also contains a significant portion of fixed-income securities and/or dividend-paying stocks provides further protection against having to sell when market conditions are unfavorable. Another example of when cash should increase in a portfolio is when the size of an individual holding becomes so large that it represents more than one-third of the total portfolio and should be reduced in size. If none of the other securities in the portfolio appear attractive on a valuation basis, cash-equivalent investments should be increased temporarily until such time as valuations improve or new candidates for investment has been identified.

In summary, it would not be unusual for a portfolio to have a cash and equivalent position of 10 percent; however, the rationale does not involve being defensive. The motivation is to be in a position to fund future commitments such as mandatory distributions, major gifts, and new investment opportunities.

Conclusions

Getting satisfactory answers to the questions listed above and observing the framework outlined in chapter 1 is my approach to identifying and investing in companies capable of generating returns exceeding that of an index fund. These tools will be less effective, however, if their use and application lacks consistency and discipline. In the decades I've been involved in managing my personal portfolio, I can identify a few instances when portfolio performance was compromised because of a failure to take action consistent with the principles I've outlined. On two occasions I failed to sell when the fundamentals at the time were in conflict with valuation, and once I sold before taking the time to recognize that improved fundamentals were right around the corner. Because of these three lapses in judgment, I'm not able to state that my results over the past twenty years or so have exceeded the returns of an index fund—even though I've come close. Perhaps this book should have been written long ago, but we can't turn back the clock. My hope and expectation is that the process of writing this book has crystallized my thinking and instilled a greater measure of patience, consistency, and discipline that I believe are and will continue to be constants for long-term individual investors.

CHAPTER 17
The Lessons of Recent History

W hen I first contemplated writing this book, I had no idea a final chapter would be needed to address the major economic events that emerged in 2008. Late in the year, the National Bureau of Economic Research officially stated that the US economy had been in a recession since December of 2007, and as the end of 2008 approached, the economic picture continued to darken, with the outlook for the housing, retail, and auto industries appearing particularly bleak. In October of 2007 the Dow Jones Industrial Average (DJIA) reached nearly 14,200. Thirteen months later the DJIA reached an intraday low of 7,450, a decline of nearly 48 percent. During this same period, the decline in the price of some stocks significantly exceeded 50 percent. For example, the stock price of General Electric—one of the few industrial companies with a AAA bond rating—declined 70 percent, and the prices of smaller companies declined even more. The collapse in equity prices was seen worldwide, and as of late December the twelve-month percentage decline in some international indices equaled or exceeded the decline of markets in the United States. The stock market is a discounting mechanism, and the decline in equity prices that occurred steadily throughout 2008 was in anticipation of one of the most severe financial crises since the Great Depression. By year's end, trillions of dollars of value had vanished from individual and institutional investment portfolios.

It's been noted that financial crises occur periodically, perhaps with surprising frequency. In every decade for the past century there's been at least one big shock to the system of a major economy. Each crisis has been unique, with varying degrees of severity, duration, and intervention by governments. The present crisis, which began in the United States and eventually spread worldwide, may prove to be one of the most severe. There's a growing consensus that the turmoil in the US financial system emerged in the latter months of 2007 but most likely had its origin in the period immediately following the 2001 recession, when over a period of four years home prices accelerated, with prices in some metropolitan areas nearly doubling. Among the consequences of rapidly rising home prices was a perception on the part of providers of mortgage credit that loans were becoming more secure, resulting in less concern about the ability of a borrower to repay the loan. Additionally, borrowers became more willing to buy larger, more expensive homes and assume the burden of higher mortgage payments. However, when home-price appreciation began to slow down, the consequences of poor underwriting and low down payments surfaced; refinancing became more difficult; and lenders tightened underwriting standards for most mortgages—but especially for those involving higher risk. The decline in home prices resulted in many borrowers being underwater, with the market prices of their homes reaching a level significantly lower than the outstanding balances of their mortgages. Also, a slowing economy and a rising unemployment rate resulted in rising mortgage payment delinquencies and foreclosures.

Superimposed on declining home prices and stressed mortgage financing is the issue of mortgage-backed securities. The concept of a mortgage-backed security (MBS) is quite simple. It represents a share of a pool of mortgages, and the principal and interest income that are paid into the pool on a regular basis become the source of income to investors. In its basic form an MBS is a pass-through instrument providing the benefit of diversification—investing in many mortgages instead of only one. When housing prices are stable or increasing and delinquency rates are low, an MBS represents a relatively secure investment. Problems arise, however, when housing prices decline and delinquency rates rise; and the major problem relates to value: what is the MBS worth, especially if it is not trading in an active market? Mortgage-backed securities and collateralized debt obligations (a variation of the MBS) were sold in huge volumes all over the world. As home prices fell and delinquencies rose, the value of these instruments not only declined but became a frequent subject of concern for chief financial officers and auditors. Markets for these securities became less active; and their estimated value required write-downs because of the highly uncertain outlook for housing and the economy. To date there have been billions of dollars of value written down involving mortgage-backed securities, and banks have been especially prominent in this regard. These write-downs required many banks to raise additional capital in an effort to maintain acceptable capital adequacy ratios, and concern for capital adequacy, in turn, caused lenders to tighten lending standards.

The financial crisis also caused businesses and consumers to improve balance sheets by restricting borrowing or even paying down debt. This deleveraging is counter-stimulative in the short run since it results in reduced spending and postpones recovery in some parts of the economy. An individual who is accelerating the pay down of debt is spending less on goods and services. A corporation paying down debt has less money for working capital and/or capital expenditures.

It is generally accepted that the deteriorating fundamentals in residential housing and the severe strains in the mortgage market, including mortgage-backed securities, played a central role in precipitating the financial crisis that remained in full force at the end of 2008 and into 2009. One school of economic thought postulates that financial crises are caused by excesses—frequently monetary excesses. In a recently published book written by John Taylor, professor of economics at Stanford University and a senior fellow at the Hoover Institution, the author states that the current crisis is no different. Monetary excesses fed the housing boom, which was followed by a bust, which in turn led to defaults, the implosion of mortgages and mortgage-related securities, and ultimately financial turmoil. The purpose of this chapter is to gain understanding rather than to assign blame for the crisis; however, it should be noted that Professor Taylor believes that his research shows that "government actions and interventions—not any inherent failure or instability of the private economy—caused, prolonged and dramatically worsened the crisis."

Two well-respected (though not widely known) academic economists, Carmen Reinhart and Kenneth Rogoff, published a book in 2009 based on research covering a period of eight centuries. The name of their book is *This Time Is Different*, but their key point is this: it's not really different. The book provides a history of financial crises in their various forms. The message of the authors is simple: we have been here before. Their research caused them to conclude that no matter how different a financial crisis may feel or appear, there are remarkable similarities with past experience both in the United States and in other countries as well.

Reinhart and Rogoff concluded that financial crises are protracted in duration and typically share three characteristics:[76]

- First, asset market price declines are deep and extended. Historically, declines in housing prices (adjusted for inflation) averaged 35 percent stretched out over six years. Four years have passed since the last peak in housing prices, and in real terms, prices of residential properties have on average declined 26 percent.

- Second, the aftermath of a banking crisis is associated with significant declines in output and employment. Historically, following a financial crisis, the unemployment rate has risen on average 7 percentage points extending over a period of about four years. Over the four years since the onset of the recession and the last low point in unemployment, the rate has risen from 4.4 to 9.1 percent (it had risen as high as 10.1 percent in October of 2009).

- Third, the amount of government debt tends to "explode" following a financial crisis; it increased an average of 86 percent (in real terms relative to precrisis debt) in the major post-WWII financial crises. America's gross debt is currently $14.3 trillion, having increased more than $1 trillion each year since 2007. The Congressional Budget Office is now projecting gross debt to exceed $20 trillion by 2020 based on current revenue and spending projections. This actual as well as anticipated increase in debt is consistent with historical experience following other crises.

It is this third characteristic—the increase in debt—that has now taken center stage with our elected representatives in Washington. A growing number of congressmen and members of the administration recognize there is an upper limit to the amount of debt this country can incur. What may be different this time is the unwillingness of rating agencies to assign the top quality rating to debt issued by the United States in the absence of fiscal discipline, and/or the reluctance of some foreign governments to increase their ownership of US government securities.

Most people, inside or outside government, no longer assume this country has an unlimited budget with which to satisfy the wishes of our friends and partners or solve all of the world's problems. It has been said that many, if not most, people in Congress and the administration know what needs to be done; the trick is in finding the right balance of initiatives that will effectively deal with the problem without weakening the political will to take action. Improving the country's balance sheet must become a national priority, even though effective action is likely to result in a temporary reduction in the long-term growth rate of economic activity.

The response to the crisis by the federal government through the Congress, US Treasury, and Federal Reserve has been broad but with mixed results to date. Lack of confidence on the part of lenders, business leaders, and consumers, and poor judgment or even mistakes on the part of government officials and policy makers acted as constraints on creating the intended impact by the various initiatives in place or contemplated. The election of a new president, Barack Obama, and the resulting change in administration also contributed to uncertainty and a delay in moving ahead with additional stimulus programs, although the Obama administration was committed to being proactive after taking office.

The financial crisis just described created a formidable backdrop of uncertainty for investors beginning in early 2008. Equity investors, in particular, dislike uncertainty, and it should come as no surprise that beginning in early May of 2008, about six months before what has recently been defined as the beginning of a recession, stock prices in nearly all segments of the equity market began a steady and continuous decline for the balance of the year. There was really no place to hide or to seek refuge. Fear took precedence over rational valuation. Short-term trading overwhelmed long-term investing. Time and again, investors who bought a stock at a new low for the year watched the share price slip even further. The most important message to investors conveyed by the comprehensive research by Reinhart and Rogoff is that economic recovery from a financial crisis involves a period of many years; five years or longer would not be an exaggeration.

The crisis resulted in legislation that produced massive federal government stimulus programs. Additionally, money was made available by the US Treasury and/or the Federal Reserve to shore up the banking system, which to varying degrees was undercapitalized. Shortly before the end of 2010, the Obama administration proposed and Congress approved the extension of the Bush tax cuts, along with various economic incentives designed to temper the impact of high unemployment, mortgage delinquencies, and residential real estate foreclosures. However, the stock market, being a discounting mechanism, early in 2009 began to reflect optimism that economic recovery would eventually occur. From March of 2009 to the end of 2010, the S&P 500 Index increased from 675 to over 1,260, a gain of 87 percent from the low. In September of 2010 the National Bureau of Economic Research determined that a trough in business activity occurred in the US economy in June, 2009, and the trough marked the end of the recession that began in December 2007. This conclusion meant the recession had lasted eighteen months, making it the longest of any recession since World War II. Similar to patterns of other business cycles, the upturn in the stock market preceded the end of the recession, in this case by three months.

In addition to the stimulus of fiscal policy, during the latter half of 2010 the Federal Reserve introduced a quantitative easing (QE) program, a government monetary policy occasionally used to increase the money supply by buying government securities or other securities from the market. Quantitative easing increases the money supply by flooding financial institutions with capital in an effort to promote increased lending, liquidity, and economic expansion. QE is controversial and is believed by some to cause inflation later in the business cycle. As this book is being written, QE is being implemented, and its consequences have yet to be determined. However, members of the Federal Reserve Board and its chairman, Ben Bernanke, believe QE is an important and useful tool and are committed to its application and eventual withdrawal when circumstances dictate it is no longer needed.

At the beginning of 2011 investors in stocks could look back at a period of financial turbulence, when conditions were such that the country could have experienced an economic calamity of historic proportions. Warren Buffett is quoted as describing the period as "an economic Pearl Harbor." However, interventions by the Obama administration, Congress, and the Federal Reserve prevented the worst from happening. But the interventions were not without cost, and looking to the future, investors are faced with another set of uncertainties. For decades our elected representatives—with the tacit backing of the majority of Americans—have seen fit to increase the size of the national budget and national debt. A number of thoughtful individuals, both inside and outside of government, continue to offer warnings regarding the unsustainability of deficit spending. A report issued in December 2010 by the National Commission on Fiscal Responsibility and Reform summed it up rather well in the preamble: "Our challenge is clear and inescapable: America cannot be great if we go broke. Our businesses will not be able to grow and create jobs, and our workers will not be able to compete successfully for the jobs of the future without a plan to get this crushing debt burden off our backs."

Every American should have on his or her required reading list "State of the Union Finances" published by the Peter G. Peterson Foundation in April of 2010. The preamble states, "The U.S. faces a looming fiscal crisis. With escalating deficits, mounting levels of public debt, growing unfunded promises for large individual entitlement programs, and increasing reliance on foreign lenders, we as U.S. citizens should be very concerned about the deteriorating financial condition of our nation."

The problems have been identified: the United States spends considerably more than it takes in; our national debt is too high, and it's growing. The solutions are complex, controversial, and challenging; they require unwavering political will to implement. The fiscal crisis, along with the threat of terrorism, international conflict, and accelerating change generally, represent formidable challenges for individual investors. However, the US economy has a reputation for resiliency, and individuals possess a spirit that looks for solutions to problems and a desire to succeed as part of a winning team. Problems to some represent opportunities for others; our history of being able to successfully deal with adversity should cause us to remain optimistic about the future. Being optimistic about the future of the United States entitles one to be excited and optimistic about investment opportunities and their rewards. I don't believe the basic requirements for investment success will change that much in the future, especially for individuals. We must be mindful of the need for patience and persistence and then buy good companies at attractive prices.

Some Important Lessons

Among the many pieces of advice I've received and given is the suggestion that one must learn from mistakes and use experiences as a platform for improving judgment and decision making. There is much that can be learned from the financial and economic crisis that emerged in 2008, and these lessons can help shape an investment framework for the future. What follows are a few of the observations and conclusions I've reached because of experience during one of the most challenging periods for the US and world economies over the past four decades:

- *It is virtually impossible to pick the bottom of a decline in the price of an individual stock or market; if that happens, it is pure luck.* Every investor has heard or used the expression, "Buy low. Sell high." Many successful investors have adhered to the philosophy of buying a stock that is out of favor, yet no investor can ever be sure when the decline in the price of a stock has run its course. Because the price of a stock on any given day is determined by a myriad of forces, one can never be certain that a purchase is being made at a level that represents a significant discount from fair value. Most buyers of goods and services are delighted when something can be purchased on sale, even though we know intuitively the item will be worth less the next day. When it comes to buying stocks, however, when we make a purchase at what we regard as an attractive price and then watch the stock decline further, our delight vanishes; it is often replaced by doubt and a reluctance to add to our position. Rejecting the notion that we can buy at the very lowest price and replacing it with the goal of trying to obtain the lowest cost in a dollar-cost averaging program seems to be an effective way of avoiding the psychological trap of being reluctant to add to a holding that you might own at a loss.

- *In a severe bear market, most valuation rules don't apply in the short run.* The forces of fear and greed are always present in equity markets. In bear markets, the forces of fear tend to dominate, and this phenomenon often results in the temporary mispricing of a stock. I believe that history will someday show us that many stocks were selling far below their intrinsic value in 2008—levels that were very inconsistent with those produced by a valuation model. When a hedge fund manager must sell to meet redemption demands or an investor has to meet a margin call, a stock sale is made at the prevailing market price, not at some predetermined price-earnings ratio, however appropriate.

- *Extreme lack of visibility and a high level of uncertainty result in highly volatile stock prices that are influenced by fear rather than fundamentals.* The prevalence of fear and greed in the market also increases stock price volatility. Emotions change rapidly during periods of uncertainty; and the tension that exists between cautious buyers and aggressive sellers oftentimes produces wide price swings as market prices seek to find equilibrium. The absence of clarity and the presence of extreme ambiguity create an environment in which speculation and a wide divergence of opinion thrive; price volatility is the inevitable by-product.

- *With respect to individual stocks, there are few if any safe havens in a severe bear market.* The Dow Jones Industrial Average may not be representative of the broad market for stocks, but it is a useful index in that it's simple and consists of large companies representing a cross-section of the economy. It's also easy to work with. A recent examination of the fifty-two-week price range of the thirty components of the DJIA provided a stunning revelation concerning the absence of safe havens in a bear market. From early February of 2008 to early February of 2009, the average decline from the fifty-two-week high to the fifty-two-week low for the thirty components of the average was 50 percent. The smallest change was Wal-Mart with a 24 percent decline; the largest change was General Motors with a 94 percent decline. Of course not all thirty stocks peaked or bottomed at the same time; however, the data speaks for itself in that bear markets can be brutal in the short run. Even defensive stocks take a significant hit.

• *High-dividend yields are not always sustainable.* Many investors believe that stocks having a long history of dividend payments represent investments with defensive characteristics; the dividend yield is viewed as limiting the downside risk in the price of a stock. However, the bear market that began in 2008 provides evidence of stocks whose prices dropped considerably more than what was expected. The dividend yield provides much less downside protection when, for whatever reason, the dividend is viewed as unsustainable.

• *Recurring revenues cushion the impact of an economic downturn.* In both the business and consumer environment, economic uncertainty causes decision makers to shift priorities and frequently scale back plans and/or reduce spending. Most business enterprises, therefore, are impacted by an economic slowdown or a recession; however, corporations that offer products and services that are essential to daily living are less sensitive to economic trends. Demand that is driven by need for replenishment or continuing service produces recurring revenues. Procter and Gamble and Kimberly-Clark are examples of companies whose products produce significant recurring revenues. Toilet paper, soap, toothpaste, cleaners, and hundreds of other nondiscretionary products cushion the impact of a recession, since revenues tend to be fairly stable, even though pricing may be subject to downward pressure. Therefore, in providing for portfolio diversification, an investor should give strong consideration to including one or more stocks of companies with significant recurring revenues.

• *The financial vitality of a company is critical, and an important metric defining financial strength is a low ratio of debt to total capital.* If there is only one lesson to be learned from the recent economic meltdown and near collapse of the global financial system, it is the critical importance of financial staying power.

Some professional investors have made and will continue to make high returns on stocks of corporations that have gotten into trouble financially, but betting on a financial turnaround is not a suitable strategy for the average investor. Avoiding big mistakes is an important tenet of successful investing. There is enough uncertainty to deal with besides financial risk, and there are hundreds of stock investment alternatives involving well-capitalized companies. Moreover, the company with financial strength is the one in a better position to capitalize on the opportunities that inevitably surface during a recession.

As outlined in the discussion of financial vitality in chapter 7, a strong balance sheet reflects a conservative use of debt, or in some cases no debt at all. But financial staying power involves other attributes such as generous cash reserves, above-average working capital, and positive cash flow. Companies with weak financial positions that were confronted by the challenges of the financial meltdown experienced an extremely sharp decline in the prices of their stocks, and in some cases were forced to raise equity capital at distressed prices.

- *Major economic events have an impact on the human psyche.* Few people would argue with the statement that the recession of 2008–09 was one of the most severe economic downturns in the past one hundred years. And for some companies (and investors as well), it may have felt like the most traumatic ever. A logical question to ask, given the severity of the recent recession, is, what will the behavioral consequences be? That is, how will people from all walks of life react? As a way of simplifying the approach to addressing this issue, let's consider three broad groups of individuals: investors, consumers, and politicians. The behaviors of all three groups have a unique and sometimes profound effect on financial markets.

Investors are a group that displays the first reaction to an economic downturn. Offered as evidence is the typical pattern of stocks declining before a recession occurs; somehow, prior to the onset of a recession, the collective actions of investors negatively impact equity prices. Significant market declines are not always followed by a recession; however, there has never been an instance in this century when a recession was not preceded by a decline in the stock market. Moreover, investors continue to have a negative impact on equity prices for some time during the decline in economic activity; however, the typical pattern is for stock prices to recover before the economy, which is the reason why stock prices are regarded as a leading indicator. Thus we can conclude that prior to and during a recession investor behavior changes, reflecting caution, pessimism, and a more defensive attitude regarding individual stocks and the market generally.

As stock market prices decline, the behavior of consumers often begins to change. Individuals become more cautions about spending money, especially on big ticket items; buying decisions are deferred in response to a concern that the stock market is signaling the beginning of a recession and possibly a rise in unemployment. The longer the decline in stock prices the more likely that consumer confidence measures will turn down, which will negatively impact the attitude and confidence of businessmen. At some point we can see evidence of a vicious circle – stock market decline – economic decline – further market decline.

Politicians react to their constituents. As the decline in stock prices begins to work its way through the economy, and as questions begin to surface regarding the direction of the unemployment rate, politicians begin to reassure their voters that a safety net of benefits is in place and will be utilized. Following the 2008-09 recession more concern has been expressed about how the promised benefits will be paid for. At some point preceding or during a recession, investors, consumers and politicians are all on the same page of pessimism, thereby setting the stage for a more significant decline in stock prices.

Ramifications for the Future

Although the severity and duration of an economic decline has a significant bearing on the pain it inflicts on investors, consumers, and politicians, there is a striking similarity in human reaction to and the psychological impact of economic recessions. Given that assumption, one could conclude that the lessons learned as a result of the 2008–09 recession are very similar to the lessons provided by prior economic downturns; and while we will vividly remember these lessons for a while and adjust our attitudes and behavior accordingly, the passage of time will result in future actions leading to excesses and subsequent correction. In my research for this chapter I came across an excerpt from a paper written by Dean Mathey, who among other things was the successful chairman of the investment committee at Princeton from the 1920s to the 1940s. The excerpt is entitled "What I Learned from the Depression." Leading off his list of lessons learned was this statement: "That once in about every 7 to 10 years there is a period of excessive general speculation culminating in a severe panic or depression when the man that is borrowing money is at a great disadvantage and he who has ready cash stands like a tower, four square to the ill winds that blow." It is interesting, indeed, that in January of 2010, in testimony before a congressional committee, Jamie Dimon, chairman and CEO of JP Morgan Chase, stated that no one should have been surprised by the events of 2008 and 2009 because "we know we have a [financial] crisis every five to ten years."

If history is a valid indicator of what we can expect in the future, there will be more recessions, and they will reveal most of the lessons of 2008 and 2009 as well as prior recessions. However, a major recession in the future may involve dynamics, conditions, and constraints of an unprecedented nature. In 2009 the Research Foundation of the CFA Institute published a collection of papers titled *Insights into the Global Financial Crisis*. The title of the lead article in that publication, written by research director Laurence Siegel, was "First Thoughts." The author acknowledged that the economy was showing signs of turning and indicated that he expected the recovery to be productive and robust. However, Mr. Siegel also made a statement that caught my eye and triggered a deep concern. His thesis was that economic risk will not go away as the economy improves. To the contrary, he believes that, because of ever-increasing government spending, there is more risk in the system than ever before. He defines the risk in this way: "The risk, simply stated, is that the *next* massive expansion of government needed (or perceived to be needed) to combat the *next* global financial crisis may not be numerically possible." Another way of saying this is that next time the US government may not have access to the financial resources required to adequately intervene and turn the economy around; the scale of resources required to make a difference will be unattainable. Were this to occur, the consequences would be incomprehensible, and the impact on stock prices impossible to imagine.

There's a glimmer of hope, however. The results of a survey conducted in April of 2010 involving high-ranking economic officials from both political parties reflect unanimous agreement that there will be another US economic crisis within ten years unless there is immediate action taken with respect to the country's structural deficit. Required action includes spending cuts and increased taxes.[77] Recognition of a problem is step one; following through with actions is the next step our elected leaders must take.

Endnotes

1. Josef Lakonishok, Andrei Shleifer, and Robert Vishny, "Contrarian Investment, Extrapolation and Risk," *Journal of Finance* 49, no. 5 (1994): 1541–78.

2. Harry Quarls, Thomas Pernsteiner, and Kasturi Rangan, "Love Your Dogs," *strategy+business* 43 (2006): 1–8.

3. David Dremen, *Contrarian Investment Strategy* (New York: Random House, 1979), 109–13.

4. Ben Stein and Phil DeMuth, *Yes, You Can Time the Market!* (Hoboken: John Wiley and Sons, 2003), 34–35.

5. Joel Greenblatt, *The Little Book That Beats the Market* (Hoboken: John Wiley & Sons, 2006). Greenblatt offers a comprehensive discussion of the Magic Formula and its application.

6. While unrelated to the corporate charter, the long history of the St. Paul and its reputation for paying all legitimate claims, including those filed following the San Francisco earthquake and fire in 1906, did make a difference in the marketplace for decades, particularly in the minds of sophisticated insurance buyers.

7. Michael Porter, "What is Strategy?" *Harvard Business Review* (November 1996).

8. Gary Hamel and C. K. Prahalad, *Competing for the Future*, (Boston: Harvard Business School Press, 1994), 221–33.

9. Peter F. Drucker, *Managing for Results* (New York: Harper and Row, 1964), 146–47.

10. James C. Collins and Jerry Porras, *Built to Last* (New York: Harper Business, 1994), 150–59.

11. Huston and Sakkab, "Connect and Develop: Inside Procter and Gamble's New Model for Innovation," *Harvard Business Review* (March 2006): 58.

12. The PWC survey was mailed to senior executives in 1,000 companies. Of the responses, 37 percent were from manufacturing companies and 63 percent from service companies. Only companies with revenues in excess of £100 million were included in the survey.

13. In addition to trust, other important characteristics are a more active flow of ideas; few organizational levels between executives and customers; and an explicit idea-management process to which people adhere.

14. Another reason for monitoring this metric is the failure rate of innovation. Research indicates that between 40 and 90 percent of new products fail to gain market acceptance. Therefore, a high percentage of revenues being generated by new offerings is an indicator of a very productive innovation process.

15. Philip Kotler, *Kotler on Marketing* (New York: Free Press, 1999). Kotler offers a comprehensive discussion of branding in chapter 4.

16. Court, Freeling, Leiter, and Parsons, "Uncovering the Value of Brands," *McKinsey Quarterly*, no. 4 (1996): 176–78.

17. Jagdish Sheth and Rajendra Sisodia, *The Rule of Three* (New York: Free Press, 2002). The book make a compelling case for accepting the rule of three as a phenomenon that can be found in nearly every aspect of business, and the authors provide examples from many industries.

18. Chris Zook with James Allen, *Profit from the Core* (Boston: Harvard Business School Press, 2001).

19. Philip Kotler, *Kotler on Marketing*, 121.

20. Ibid, 132–33.

21. Evan R. Hirsch and Steven B. Wheeler, "Channel Champions," *Strategy and Business* 17 (1999). Refer to this article for a more complete discussion of the topic.

22. Graham, Dodd, and Cottle, *Security Analysis, Principles and Techniques*, 4th ed., 671.

23. Kotter, *A Force For Change* (New York: Free Press, 1990). Kotter provides an insightful discussion on the differences between leadership and management.

24. This statement was made by Dr. Warren Bennis during a presentation at the Executive Roundtable, sponsored by the American Council of Life Insurance, held in Palm Springs, California, January 1992.

25. John Gardner, *On Leadership* (New York: Free Press, 1990).

26. Warren Bennis, *On Becoming a Leader* (Boston: Addison Wesley, 1989).

27. James C. Collins and Jerry Porras, *Built to Last* (New York: Harper Business, 1994. Refer to chapter 8.

28. Gary Hamel and C. K. Prahalad, *Competing for the Future* (Boston: HBS Press, 1994).

29. "Anatomy of a Healthy Corporation," *McKinsey Quarterly*, no. 3 (2007): 64–73. This comprehensive and well-researched paper published by McKinsey and Company on the subject of corporate health is the basis for my discussion of this topic. Readers are encouraged to review the piece.

30. Justin Menkes, *Executive Intelligence* (New York: HarperCollins, 2005). Refer to Menkes's book for a comprehensive discussion.

31. Philip Kotler, *Kotler on Marketing* (New York: Free Press, 1999), 36–42.

32. In September of 1982 seven people in the Chicago area died after taking capsules of Extra Strength Tylenol. In addition to the five bottles that lead to the death of the victims, several other tampered bottles were discovered. Johnson and Johnson distributed warnings to hospitals and distributors and then halted the production and advertising of Tylenol products. In early October the company issued a nationwide recall involving an estimated 31 million bottles of the product with a retail value of over $100 million. To this day, the prompt action of the company is cited as an example of how corporate values dictated the response of management and protected the welfare of the public.

33. Michael Porter, "What is Strategy?," *Harvard Business Review* (November 1996). Porter's article offers a more complete discussion of the subject.

34. McKinsey and Company, *Valuation: Measuring and Managing the Value of Companies* (New York: John Wiley and Sons, 2005). This book includes a comprehensive discussion of return on invested capital in chapter 6.

35. The equation has been empirically derived. It represents the best fit for a second-degree curve that produces an EF of 0.5 for a score of 5; an EF of 0.65 for a score of 15 (average of 3 or moderately weak); an EF of 1.0 for a score of 30 (average of 6 or moderately strong); and an EF of 1.5 for a score of 45 (an average of 9 or very strong). Intuitively, the values seem appropriate if one agrees that valuation should be discounted for weakness in a business model and assigned a premium for strength. An EF of 1.0, essentially a neutral rating, seems appropriate when the score reflects conditions that are moderately strong on average.

36. The model, which I have modified from one proposed by Benjamin Graham, takes the following form: PSR = M × [8.5 + (G1 + G2) × (4.4/BY)] × EF; where M = normalized aftertax profit margin; G1 = five-year consensus growth rate of earnings per share; G2 = growth rate for years six through ten (typically discounting G1 by at least

25 percent); BY = the greater of 7.5 percent or the current thirty-year AAA corporate bond yield; and EF = Expectation Factor unique to the company being valued. The PSR is then multiplied by the most recently reported trailing four-quarter sales per share to arrive at a fair value assumption. Use of a price-to-sales ratio provides some stability to the valuation process, especially when earnings are depressed or nonexistent, conditions which render the use of price-earnings ratios impractical.

37. The study covered a ten-year period, from 1988 to 1997 and revealed that when the median overhang from companies in the study increased from 10.6 percent to 18.7 percent, total shareholder returns declined from 16.9 percent to 13.5 percent. Another revelation was that when the median overhang declined from 10.6 percent to 5.7 percent, total shareholder returns declined less than one percent, from 16.9 percent to 16.2 percent. Source: watsonwyatt.com.

38. Jim Collins, *Good to Great* (New York: HarperCollins, 2001). In *Good to Great*, the author reveals what he describes as surprising results from extensive research looking for patterns and correlations between forms and levels of compensation and corporation performance. The conclusion was this: "We found no systematic pattern linking executive compensation to the process of going from good to great."

39. Bargeron, Schlingemann, Stulz, and Zutter, "Why Do Private Acquirers Pay So Little Compared to Public Acquirers?," *NBER Working Paper*, no. 13061 (April, 2007). In an article in the *New York Times* (May 13, 2007), Mark Hulbert suggests that when corporate managers have only a small ownership stake, they are more likely to pursue acquisitions that do not enhance shareholders' long-term value; their motivations may simply be to satisfy their egos (and/or increase compensation levels) by building a corporate empire.

40. Robert P. Miles, *The Warren Buffett CEO* (New York: John Wiley and Sons, 2002).

41. Ibid., 351.

42. Denise Dickins and Robert Houmes, "Executive Compensation: Much Ado about Nothing?," *Financial Analysts Journal* 63, no. 3 (May/June 2007): 28–31.

43. "Psychological Ownership and Feelings of Possession: Three Field Studies Predicting Employee Attitudes and Organizational Citizenship Behavior," *Journal of Organizational Behavior* 25 (2004): 439–59.

44. Message to shareholders from president and CEO Scott Edmonds, included in the 2006 annual report of Chico's FAS, Inc.

45. Barton Biggs, *Hedgehogging* (New York: John Wiley and Sons, 2006), 242–43.

46. For a comprehensive discussion of the Magic Formula approach to stock selection and portfolio management, consult Joel Greenblatt's *The Little Book That Beats the Market*. Annual returns for the period from 1988 to 2004 period are displayed in Table 7.1 on page 61.

47. Intrinsic value or fair value is the underlying perception of the value of a company based on both qualitative factors (business model, markets served, competitive advantage, quality of management) and quantitative factors (financial statement analysis). One of several approaches to calculating intrinsic value is to estimate future net cash flows (after taxes, provision for working capital and capital expenditures) discounted at a rate equal to the cost of capital for the corporation. The various qualitative and quantitative factors will, to varying degrees, influence the assumptions incorporated into the forecast of future net cash flows as well as the discount rate.

48. G. M. Loeb, *The Battle for Investment Survival* (New York: Simon and Schuster, 1957).

49. Benjamin Graham, *The Intelligent Investor,* 2nd rev. ed. (New York: Harper and Brothers, 1959), 81.

50. Richard A. Brealey, *An Introduction to Risk and Return from Common Stocks* (Boston: MIT Press, 1969).

51. Ibid., 127, Table 35.

52. Robert M. Sharp, *Calculated Risk: A Master Plan for Common Stocks* (New York: Dow Jones Irwin, 1986), 80.

53. Cris Zook with James Allen, *Profit from the Core* (Boston: Harvard Business School Press, 2001), 9–13.

54. Ernest von Simson, *The Limits of Strategy: Lessons in Leadership from the Computer* (Bloomington, IN: iUniverse, 2009).

55. Larry Bossidy and Ram Charan, *The Discipline of Getting Things Done* (New York: Crown Publishing Corporation, 2002).

56. "Briefing Procter and Gamble," *Economist* (August 11, 2007): 61–63.

57. A recent examination of the Dow Jones Industrial Average revealed an average plus or minus deviation from the mean of fifty-two-week high and low prices of about 16 percent. This variation is considered normal, and it would seem that an overvaluation benchmark should exceed normal variation by more than a factor of two. Thus, the rationale for the arbitrary choice of 50 percent.

58. James J. Valentine, CFA, *Best Practices for Equity Research Analysts* (New York: McGraw Hill, 2011).

59. In the late 1800s, economist and avid gardener Vilfredo Pareto established that 80 percent of the land in Italy was owned by 20 percent of the population. While gardening he later observed that 20 percent of the peapods in his garden yielded 80 percent of the peas that were harvested. And thus was born a theory that has stood the test of time and scrutiny. The Pareto Principle or the 80/20 Rule has proven its validity in a number of other areas, including business.

60. Robert G. Hagstrom, *The Essential Buffett: Timeless Principles for the New Economy* (New York: John Wiley and Sons, 2001).

61. Justin Menkes, *Executive Intelligence* (New York: HarperCollins, 2005).

62. Ibid.

63. John Train, *The Money Masters* (New York: Harper and Row, 1980), 213.

64. Douglas H. Bellemore, *The Strategic Investor* (New York: Simmons-Boardman, 1963).

65. Refer to the definition of the Magic Formula as listed in the appendix of Joel Greenblatt's *The Little Book That Beats the Market*.

66. Peter F. Drucker, *Managing for Results* (New York: Harper and Row, 1964), 3–14. Drucker provides a more comprehensive discussion of business realities on these pages.

67. Alan Greenspan, "The Globalization of Finance," *Cato Journal* 17, no. 3. This is an edited version of a keynote address by Alan Greenspan on October 14, 1997.

68. Alan Greenspan, *The Age of Turbulence* (New York: Penguin, 2007). Refer to chapter 19.

69. "Exchanges Benefit from Record Volumes," BusinessWeek Online, July 28, 2007.

70. James Montier, *Behavioral Finance* (New York: John Wiley and Sons, 2002). See chapter 1.

71. Ben Stein, "Everybody's Business," *New York Times*, January 27, 2009.

72. Malcolm Gladwell, *Blink* (New York: Little, Brown, 2005).

73. Mary Buffett and David Clark, *The Tao of Warrant Buffett* (New York: Scribner, 2006), 28.

74. Michael Porter, "The Five Competitive Forces That Shape Strategy," *Harvard Business Review* (January 2008). Refer to this article for the most recent insights concerning the competitive forces that impact an industry's structure and profitability. Mr. Porter first introduced the concept of five forces in 1979, and his work has influenced a generation of academic research and business practice. A key point in this recent article by Porter is that industry structure

drives competitive behavior and profitability regardless of industry profile or type.

75. The forecast model is as follows: Price = EPS × (8.5 + 2 × Growth Rate) × (4.4/AAA bond rate)

76. Carmen M. Reinhart and Kenneth S. Rogoff, *This Time Is Different* (Princeton, NJ: Princeton University Press, 2009), 223–24.

77. See the Peter G. Peterson Foundation news release dated April 26, 2010, at www.pgpf.org.

Made in the USA
Lexington, KY
30 April 2012